"...so help me, God"

THE U.S. PRESIDENTS IN PERSPECTIVE

"...so help me, God"

THE U.S. PRESIDENTS IN PERSPECTIVE

Daniel Ernest White

Nova Science Publishers, Inc.

New York

Art Director: Maria Ester Hawrys
Assistant Director: Elenor Kallberg
Graphics: Denise Dieterich, Kerri Pfister,
         Erika Cassatti and Barbara Minerd
Manuscript Coordinator: Gloria H. Piza
Book Production: Tammy Sauter, and Gavin Aghamore
Circulation: Irene Kwartiroff and Annette Hellinger

Library of Congress Cataloging-in-Publication Data

White, Daniel Ernest.
So help me God: the U.S. presidents in perspective/ Daniel
E. White.
       p. cm.
    Includes bibliographical references.
    ISBN 1-56072-334-3 :
    1. Presidents--United States. 2. Presidents--United States-
-Inauguration. 3. Presidents--United States--Religion. I. Title.
 JK516.W48 1996   96-23829
 324.6'3'0973--dc20   ·   CIP

© 1996 Nova Science Publishers, Inc.
  6080 Jericho Turnpike, Suite 207
  Commack, New York 11725
  Tele. 516-499-3103 Fax 516-499-3146
  E Mail Novasci1@aol.com

Printed in the United States of America

To Judy,
my wife and collaborator,
whose idea this was.

$\mathcal{C}ontents$

Introduction

I swear, so help me God.

George Washington added these six words upon completing the
Constitutionally prescribed oath of office in 1789. Forty other
Americans have followed his example as they became President of the
United States. Some of the forty came to office filled with anxiety,
especially those who advanced because of the death of their predecessor.
Others have called their inaugurations a new beginning for the nation, a
political hyperbole usually accompanied by much joy and celebration. In
all instances, our American political tradition has been for Presidents to
ask for aid from a Higher Source at the start.

President Washington's appeal for divine help in the midst of a
political setting both sustained a tradition and established a new one.
The earliest document of political importance in America was the
Mayflower Compact, an agreement among 41 passengers "like the
church covenant by which the Separatists formed congregations, except
that it set up a civil government..." The first words of the Compact are
"In the Name of God, Amen."

Later, the first significant American writer, Governor John
Winthrop, extolled the virtues of the new land and called upon America
to become like a City on a Hill, a beacon to the rest of the world. And
what did Winthrop propose as the underlying philosophy in this
exemplar society? Read Micah 6:8, a verse used by at least two
Presidents in their oath-taking ceremonies: "What does the Lord require

of you, but to do justice, love mercy and walk humbly with thy God."
Winthrop's vision was a just and merciful society submissive to the will
of God.

The Pilgrims of Plymouth and the Puritan Governor Winthrop
might be expected to be routine in their references to the Almighty.
Thomas Jefferson was no Puritan, not a clergyman and not much of a
church-goer. Yet, even Jefferson connected the civil and the religious in
one of the most well-known sentences in American history: "...endowed
by their Creator with certain unalienable rights, among these life, liberty
and the pursuit of happiness."

President Washington warned, "let us with caution indulge the
supposition that morality can be sustained without religion." [1] While
citizens and historians might debate the presence or absence of morality
throughout our nation's history, none can argue the fact that among the
words and symbols present as our nation's highest political office has
passed from one to another are the Bible and the words, *I swear, so help
me God*, sustaining an historical link between civil and religious life in
America.

For much of British history, kings and queens have taken oaths on
the Bible as they were coronated. Symbolically, perhaps, President
Washington swore on an open Bible, establishing a new American
tradition. For Washington, the Bible was opened at random, and many
of his successors followed suit. Others have chosen specific verses or
books of the Bible. The reasons for a particular choice are as varied as
the men who have occupied the office. Interestingly enough, more than
twice as many have chosen Old Testament verses as New Testament
ones, and the Psalms have been used more than any other book.
Perhaps the position of the Psalms at the center of many Bibles
explains the choice; triumphant Presidents choosing joyful texts is
another explanation.

If the President did choose, what verse or chapter has the new Chief
Executive chosen? Has that choice carried special meaning, either to
the President himself or in revealing something about the historical
context in which the oath was taken? Was a random selection
particularly apt? Was the Bible significant to the President's life or was
religion of little importance to him? Was a verse prophetic? Does a
reference in an Inaugural Address reveal something about the President

and his religious faith? "... so *help me God*"addresses these questions and looks at each inauguration for its unique aspects.

All but two of our Presidents have elected to *swear* the oath; those two chose to *affirm*. Columnist William Safire noted in 1985 that "the Chief Justice always asks, do you want to swear or affirm...piety is approved but must never be demanded...an oath before God is a matter of choice, not necessity." (2) Such sensitivity is appropriate for a nation free of an established church. We enjoy a rich tradition in America of religious freedom, protected by the Constitutional separation of church and state. All the more significant, then, that the last words spoken by an American before becoming President are, by tradition and custom, "I swear, so help me God."

George Washington

Genesis 49 and 50 tells of Jacob at the end of his life describing to his sons "that which shall befall you in the last days." He details the fate of the twelve tribes of Israel, then breathes no more, son Joseph falling upon him, weeping. Joseph, Jacob's favorite in the jealous eyes of his brothers, was sold into bondage in Egypt but rose to be the favored one of the Pharaoh, making it possible for him to take his father to bury him in the land of Canaan, the promised land.

George Washington's hand rested on this part of Genesis when he became the first to recite the thirty-six words prescribed in Article Two of the Constitution as the oath of office. He added six more words: "I swear, so help me God." Then Washington kissed the Bible. Those words and that action, as did every other aspect of the first inauguration, set precedents which generally have been followed ever since. Following the oath-taking, President Washington delivered the first Inaugural Address.

In it Washington never used the word *God*; for he was a deist, believing in a divine force but one without name or definition. However, nearly one third of this first inaugural address in American history was composed of religious references. "Almighty Being," "great Author of every public and private good," "Providential agency;" these phrases make clear Washington's belief that success for the new nation and its new President depended in a significant way on the blessings and grace of God. [3]

The Bible was Washington's idea, though the book was not his. Rather, this copy of the Holy Scriptures was borrowed from St. John's Lodge, Free and Accepted Masons, and has been used several times since. The Bible was held by Secretary of the Senate Samuel Allyne Otis, who opened it at random. But what a fortuitous opening!

The new nation which elected Washington its first leader, has laid claim to many of the fates seen by Jacob for his sons; the bountiful harvests of Asher, the blessings of good land given to Issachar, the strength and might of Joseph. And, certainly, in recent centuries, America has been the new Canaan, the land of promise for the people of many nationalities.

Beloved by the people, some say they were ready to make Washington king. But, in the events leading up to his inauguration and as President, Washington conducted himself as the servant of the people. He saw himself as a citizen like any other, now temporarily invested with the power and responsibility of governing. Many were the opportunities to be elevated and the foreign governments represented at his inauguration gave Washington countless examples of how excessive majesty could be injected into our system. His choice of "Mr. President" as the way the President would be addressed -- rather than Your Highness or Excellency -- illustrates Washington's keen understanding of how the United States was to be unique among the nations in the 18th century.

Washington was not inaugurated on March 4 as was the practice until 1937, but on April 30, 1789. Weather played a major role in the delay. The results of the first meeting of the Electoral College could not be received by Congress until they achieved a quorum, and that did not happen until April 6. Of course, everyone knew the outcome. But following the prescribed form, Washington waited to be officially informed before setting out for the nation's capital.

That capital was New York in 1789. Washington's second inauguration was in Philadelphia in 1793. Thereafter, except in cases of death of the incumbent, all other inaugural ceremonies have been in Washington D.C. Following his speech in New York, Washington joined others in the inaugural party for a worship service at St. Paul's Chapel, Episcopal. Though most of his successors have attended services on Inauguration Day, Washington has been the only President to include that worship as an official part of the ceremony.

Appropriately so, for while Washington clearly wanted to secure the blessings of God to accompany the blessing of liberty, he was also mindful that ours was a land of no established religion. Shortly after his taking office, Washington and his contemporary politicians made clear the official separation of church and state through the First Amendment of the Constitution. Significantly, however, they recognized that proscribing an established church did not preclude piety as a part of the assumption of great responsibility. Washington's precedents took root.

President Washington's second inauguration was remarkable only for the brevity of his address; 135 words, the shortest ever. No record was made of the scripture verses to which the Bible was opened, but that it was under his left hand as he recited the oath a second time is, given the events of 1789, a virtual certainty.

Washington presided for eight years, during which time our borders were secured, our currency fixed and supported, our capital founded and our place among sovereign nations established. Like Joseph of old, "the archers have sorely grieved him (Washington), and shot at him and hated him. But his bow abode in strength and the alms of his hands were made strong by the mighty God of Jacob..."(Gen. 49:23-24) And, the inhabitants of this new Canaan, our promised land, have prospered. Thanks be to God, and George Washington!

John Adams

66 "The most perfect philosophy, the most perfect morality, and the most refined policy." With these words to Benjamin Rush, John Adams described the contents of the Bible. [4] He declared it was "the most republican book in the world" because "in its commandments were to be found the only preservative of republics." Given that respect for the Bible, the precedents set by Washington, and the practice of the British monarchs before, it is likely that Adams took the oath of office with his hand on the book he valued so much.

President Adams wrote to his wife on the evening of March 4, 1797, "Your dearest friend never had a more trying day." Odd words for one just installed as President. Yet John Adams endured the fate of being the successor to the Father of his country. He took up his duties in Philadelphia deprived of the company of Abigail, his wife and "dearest friend." Not much thought was given in 1797 to bringing a wife to live in the capital city; it just wasn't an issue. Thus, through letters Adams described the sense of triumph at achieving the presidency and the deep sense of both duty and caution which made him approach the office as the undertaking of an ordeal.

John Adams grew up in a devout family in the Puritan community of Braintree, Massachusetts. In adulthood, his own religious beliefs blended his consistent intellectualism with the Puritan tradition in Unitarianism, a movement centered in his homestate. First a teacher, then a lawyer, he began his career in public service as a member of the

Continental Congress in 1774 and thereafter drew a government salary until his retirement from the presidency in 1801. More of a philosopher than Washington, Adams was one of the first public figures to adopt the idea of a complete break from England and in 1776, he argued vigorously for the Declaration of Independence in Congress. He spent many of the years prior to his Vice Presidency under Washington as the U.S. representative to various nations of Europe, becoming one of our early experts in foreign affairs.

Adams understood his inauguration to represent a unique moment in history. The Presidency was changing hands for the first time, a fact he noted to Abigail: "the sight of the sun setting full-orbed and another rising, was a novelty." As might be expected, given Washington's stature, Adams was, to some extent, overshadowed at his own inauguration. Yet a contemporary observed that the United States "should lose nothing by the change," so well-respected were Adams' mind and his record of successful public service. [5]

In his Inaugural Address, after taking the oath from the first Chief Justice of the United States, Oliver Ellsworth, President Adams traced the movement toward independence, the critical period under the Articles of Confederation, and the drafting of the Constitution. Then he praised the first government as meeting all of the hopes of the framers of the Constitution and applauded George Washington's performance as President. Adams followed with a pledge "to honor the law and letter of the constitution," a promise quite in keeping with his training in the law. Speaking plainly about the major political issue of the day, U.S. attitudes toward France and England as those European nations fought again, Adams pledged himself to work for peace through American neutrality. He concluded by saying that he would do his best to support the constitution with the blessing of Almighty God.

President Adams sought continuity and unity. Instead, under his administration, political positions rigidified and parties coalesced around Federalist and anti-Federalist orientations. By the close of his term, an odious Sedition Act, punishing criticism of the government, was passed, set to expire the day before the inauguration of the next President, in case Adams' side lost. The law was being used to blunt the guarantees of the Constitution and was itself the cause of bitter public debate. Adams, the first Vice President to become President, became in 1800 the first incumbent President to be defeated for re-election.

Adams retired to Braintree, to read, write and philosophize. The Enlightenment assertion of the perfectibility of man drew particular criticism from the ex-President. Only through devotion to God as revealed through the Bible, argued Adams, could man gain wisdom and order in his life. Only through adherence to God's laws would man avoid misery and calamity. One imagines John Adams satisfied on March 4, 1797, swearing to preserve, protect and defend the Constitution on the book of the laws of his God, the ultimate source of wisdom for mankind.

Thomas Jefferson

"And when he had made a scourge of small cords, he drove them all out of the temple, and the sheep, and the oxen; and poured out the changers' money, and overthrew the tables; And he said unto them that sold the doves, Take these things hence; make not my Father's house an house of merchandise." (John 2: 15-16) Thomas Jefferson might well have sworn his oath of office on these verses, for his election in 1800 was viewed by his opponents as "the Revolution of 1800," an overthrow of the established (though only twelve years so) order by a Francophile, a democrat and an anti-Christian.

They are also the first actions taken by the adult Jesus of Nazareth in *The Jefferson Bible*. Our third Chief Executive was the only President to write his own version of the Gospels. Cutting out references to Jesus' divinity and passages he believed the result of subsequent writers putting words in Jesus' mouth, Jefferson constructed a Bible which intertwined the stories of Matthew, Mark, Luke and John into a single narrative. He wrote because, in his words, "to the corruptions of Christianity I am indeed opposed; but not to the genuine precepts of Jesus himself."

Jefferson's elevation to the Presidency sparked heated passions. In a political system not conceived to support political parties, Jefferson emerged as the leader of the party in opposition to that of George Washington and John Adams. In an administration under Adams which threatened war with France over various disputes, Jefferson, though Vice

President, openly supported the French. They had supported our revolutionary effort and their revolution derived from the same democratic passions as did ours. Whereas Adams and the Federalists preferred rule by the aristocracy, Jefferson believed the people, the common man, could be trusted with self-rule.

Small wonder, then, that President Adams chose not to attend the first presidential inauguration to take place in Washington D.C. on March 4, 1801. Though he and Jefferson had been personal and political friends through the early years of the United States and would reconcile years later, in 1801 Adams believed that the country faced doom. Jefferson's politics frightened Adams for the nation; the Virginian advocated states' rights, opposed the National Bank, envisioned a nation not of capitalists but of "yeoman farmers," and supported extensions of the right to vote. Adams thought Jefferson a potential demagogue.

Even the election bred controversy. In the Electoral College, Jefferson and Aaron Burr tied for the Presidency. The Constitution prescribed resolution in the House of Representatives. There, the vote of the state of New York proved crucial. That vote depended upon the influence of another prominent Federalist, Alexander Hamilton. Hamilton chose Jefferson as the lesser of two evils, laying the groundwork for the duel fought by Burr and Hamilton in 1803.

Jefferson's religious beliefs provoked as well. A part of his youth Jefferson spent living in the household of a strict Anglican clergyman who delighted in defending the established religion of Virginia. Jefferson chafed under this imposed orthodoxy and developed a healthy distaste both for those who would demand that others believe without question and for those who twisted "a system of morals...the most perfect and sublime that has ever been taught by man" (taught by Jesus) for their own denominational or institutional purposes. His Bill for Establishing Religious Freedom, adopted by Virginia in 1786, ranked among his three most significant accomplishments, if one judged by the epitaph on his tombstone which he wrote. The roots of the bill were in his youth.

A deist, believing in the Creator God but not in His intervention in the lives of believers, Jefferson corresponded with leading men of his time about the Christian religion and the teachings of Jesus. These writings culminated in his own attempt at a religious book, *The Jefferson Bible*. Underlying his work was the same indefatigable belief in the value of individual human beings, as capable of moral action by reading and interpreting the "real Jesus" as they were of self-government.

His first inauguration modeled "Republican simplicity" as he called it, forsaking distinctions of rank or decoration. Jefferson delivered his address softly. Few actually heard the speech but those who did found it conciliatory and reassuring. "We are all Democrats, we are all Federalists" was particularly calming. Jefferson's cousin, Chief Justice John Marshall, administered the oath of office. Then Jefferson walked back to his hotel for lunch.

By the time of his second inauguration, Jefferson lived at the Executive Mansion, far enough away from the Capitol so that he rode his horse to the event. He gave his speech, took his oath and returned to the White House because he had invited visitors to tour the building during the rest of that day and evening. Already by 1805, under President Jefferson's leadership, the nation had made the Louisiana Purchase, won a small naval war in the Mediterranean and proclaimed to the world its neutral rights in the new fight between England and France. Yet Jefferson's simplicity of personal and professional demeanor broadcast democratic virtue.

Perhaps Jefferson's inaugural Bible in 1805 would have been opened to Matthew 5, the first sermon preached by Jesus in *The Jefferson Bible*. "Blessed are the poor in spirit...blessed are the meek...blessed are ye when men shall revile you...rejoice and be exceeding glad: for great is your reward in heaven." Revolutionary, statesman, philosopher, deist, controversial politician, architect, musician, inventor, author of the Declaration of Independence; Jefferson was these and more, a genius, a giant among men. "Republicanism is a part of the truth of Christianity," wrote Jefferson to Rev. Jeremy Belknap in 1791. "It abolishes the false glare which surrounds kingly government..." [6] Jefferson, the reviled, the meek, the poor in spirit; how fortunate the nation to have him establish the standard for transition in the Presidency from one political philosophy to another. Demonstrating that our nation could still be united, in spite of clashing views, might be Jefferson's greatest among his many gifts to his country.

James Madison

The Revolutionary War, the Declaration of Independence and the Constitution and Bill of Rights dominated the history of the United States in the last quarter of the 19th century. By 1808, the winning general and the author of the Declaration had each won two terms as President of the new nation. The election of 1808 elevated the third great person associated with these dominant events, James Madison, the "Father of the Constitution." The scholarly Madison, Jefferson's Secretary of State and intellectual as well as political disciple, became the fourth President on March 4, 1809 and despite a divisive war with Britain, took the oath a second time in 1813.

On the first occasion, Madison was acutely aware that he followed in office a great man. Thomas Jefferson was equally cognizant that there was potential for detracting from the newly elected President if the outgoing Chief Executive was too visible. Thus, accounts of the day detail several self-effacing actions by Jefferson: sitting with the Virginia delegation at the oath-taking rather than in front, leaving the Capitol after the President's party had departed and by himself, and slipping away from the Inaugural Ball after arriving early so as to be the first to greet the Madisons.

As with others in those early times, the inauguration in 1809 featured some "firsts." For example, the militia offered to ride escort for Madison from his home to the Capitol, thus constituting the first inaugural parade. Mr. Madison wore clothing all items of which were made in the USA. And in the evening, due to the influence of Dolley Madison, a gala ball was held, a high society affair which set a precedent for inaugural balls.

Madison emulated Washington by taking the oath of office first then making his speech. Chief Justice John Marshall officiated. Madison followed with an address clear in its political and philosophical consistency with his predecessor. While there is no specific mention in historical accounts of an open Bible or favorite verse, President Madison continued and embellished upon a practice evident in the first presidential utterances of predecessors and successors alike. In concluding his first inaugural speech, Madison conjoined the blessings and power of God with the wisdom and power of the American people.

President Madison described the people as "the source to which I look for the aids which alone can supply my deficiencies...the well-tried intelligence and virtue of my fellow citizens." His next and final sentence was: "In these my confidence will...be best placed, next to that which we have all been encouraged to feel in the guardianship and guidance of that Almighty Being whose power regulates the destiny of nations, whose blessings have been so conspicuously dispensed to this rising Republic, and to whom we are bound to address our devout gratitude for the past, as well as our fervent supplication and best hopes for the future." Regularly, in inaugurations to come, there would appear this same explicit claim of God's favor reflected in the advancing prosperity of the nation.

Not, however, in the inauguration of 1813. Then, war with Britain, a war opponents called "Mr. Madison's War," elicited from the President bold defenses of his policies in the face of uneven military results. While American naval forces had won the day several times, our land troops were being thrashed at Detroit, Ft. Dearborn and Ft. George, among other places. The burning of Washington D.C. was to follow in 1814. Madison suggested that winning the war would require the "smiles of Heaven." This blessing was not forthcoming. The truce confirmed in 1815 by the Treaty of Ghent produced no victory for either side. The war made Madison very unpopular but peace helped. His Secretary of State, and later Secretary of War as well, James Monroe, won the presidential election of 1816 easily.

Dolley Madison did ensure that the second Inauguration would be festive, though. She came to the Executive Mansion with a well-established reputation as a hostess and offered many opportunities for merriment at the Mansion during the first term. Not surprisingly the Inaugural Ball in 1813 matched the first in elegance and social comment. The ball highlighted an otherwise routine day, if inaugurations can ever be routine, in which the militia took the President to the Capitol, the Chief Justice administered the oath and the President spoke, for less time on this occasion.

The travails of the second term, however, could not dimish the importance of Madison's contribution to religion in America. In his work on the Bill of Rights, Madison wrote freedom of religion into the First Amendment. As author Garry Wills has observed, Madison's desire to keep church and state separate were for reasons quite like those of the most famous advocate of separation, the 17th century founder of Rhode Island, Roger Williams. [7] Williams founded the colony on the belief that the state should not intrude upon the affairs of religion; therefore religion and state must be kept separate.

Freedom to believe as one wanted became a cornerstone to the First Amendment and, in Madison's view, if the freedom were to be violated, it would be "an offense against God not against man." Without an established state religion in America, many denominations and faiths have followed.

Like Jefferson, James Madison idealized a Christianity of a former time, before centuries of church interpretations overlaid the faith. But Christian he was, on many occasions affirming the value of spreading the gospel. To preserve his right and the right of every other American to follow the faith of his or her choice, Madison defended the separation of church and state over the whole of his lifetime. "Render unto Caesar the things that are Caesar's and unto God the things that are God's" preached Jesus (Matthew 22:21) James Madison well understood the message.

James Monroe

In 1820 one person in the Electoral College voted for John Quincy Adams. The rest voted for James Monroe. The man who voted for Adams said that only George Washington should ever receive a unanimous vote. The balloting revealed two facts: after the demise of the Federalist Party, it took some time for a second party to emerge. And, James Monroe was very highly regarded. Thomas Jefferson said Monroe was "a man whose soul might be turned wrong side outward, without discovering a blemish to the world." [8]

When James Monroe swore "to preserve, protect and defend the Constitution" on March 4, 1817, he became the fourth and last of the "Virginia dynasty", a group prominent in the founding of the nation, to take the presidency. Like Washington, Monroe had fought in the war, sustaining a wound at Trenton but earning the rank of major by age 19. During the final stages of the war, he studied law under Thomas Jefferson and was one of his successors as Governor of Virginia. Monroe served James Madison as Secretary of State and Secretary of War and he served terms in both the U.S. Senate and the Virginia House of Delegates. Indeed, his political ancestry was impressive.

Monroe took the oath of office from a man with whom he had spent considerable time in his youth, Chief Justice John Marshall. This inauguration was the first to be held outdoors in Washington, D.C., on the east side of the Capitol. As a result, the crowd was the largest in history to that date. Warm and sunny weather added to the sense that all was well with the young republic. Indeed, historians now refer to the days of the first Monroe Administration as the "Era of Good Feelings."

Before the oath, Monroe delivered his address, written "in a plain style of writing," according to one observer. [9] As he outlined his hopes for a stronger central government and a national bank, he also spoke of the United States' role in defense of the whole of the Western hemisphere; it should, Monroe argued, be for the exclusive use of Americans, North and South respectively. He concluded: " Relying on the aid to be derived from the other departments of the government, I enter on the trust to which I have been called by the suffrages of my fellow citizens with my fervent prayers to the Almighty that He will be graciously pleased to continue to us that protection which He has already so conspicuously displayed in our favor."

This sentence is one of the few ever uttered publicly by Monroe which gave evidence of his religious beliefs. Though he was a lifelong Episcopalian, Monroe, in the words of one biographer, "was extremely reticent as to his religious sentiments, at least in all that he wrote. Allusions to his beliefs are rarely, if ever, to be met with in his correspondence." [10] A contemporary engraving of that March day in 1817 shows Monroe's hand on a book, and since there is specific evidence that the Vice President swore his oath on the Bible, likely Monroe did so as well. After all, he was not the type to break the traditions established by the first President.

As President, Monroe made his mark in foreign affairs. He signed the treaty with England establishing the 49th parallel as the boundary with Canada, and the Adams-Onis Treaty adding Florida to the U.S. While his name is attached to the U.S. policy followed in our relations with the rest of the Western hemisphere, the policy itself was probably the work of his Secretary of State, John Qunicy Adams.

President Monroe is also the only American Chief Executive to have a foreign capital named after him, Monrovia, Liberia. That honor occurred because of his visible support for the work of the American Colonization Society which returned freed blacks to Africa. In 1820, President Monroe signed the Missouri Compromise which established a geographical limit to the spread of slavery in hopes that the passions of the citizenry over the issue might be cooled. Such a reaction is consistent with the words used repeatedly to describe Monroe:

industrious, serious, reflective, temperate with great natural dignity, deliberate in forming opinions.

President Monroe's second inauguration, after the stunning vote in the Electoral College, produced another first. March 4, 1821 fell on a Sunday. Out of respect for the Sabbath, the inauguration was delayed a day. But the President's first term expired at noon on the 4th anyway as did the Vice President's. By Act of Congress, in the event the two offices fell vacant, the President Pro-Tempore of the Senate became President. Consequently, for one day, Senator John Guillard of South Carolina technically served as President, the only one-day President in our history.

March 5 proved such a dismal day that the ceremonies were moved indoors. Once again, President Monroe delivered his inaugural address before taking the oath of office, and he repeated many of the same themes from his first address. Only, he took longer, longer than most other Presidents before or since.

In one passage, though, President Monroe makes clear his love of the union, only a few months after signing the Missouri Compromise, designed to calm the heated passions over the balance of free and slave states. "...It is obvious that other powerful causes, indicating the great strength and stability of our Union, have essentially contributed to draw you together. That these powerful causes exist, and that they are permanent, is my fixed opinion; that they may produce a like accord in all questions touching, however remotely, the liberty, prosperity and happiness of our country will always be the object of my most fervent prayers to the Supreme Author of all Good." Of course, the permanence of those "unifying causes" would be severely threatened in less than a generation's time.

President Monroe provided a good example of how important the ritual call for divine guidance has been at the start of American presidential administrations. No one was more reticent to speak publicly about his religious beliefs than James Monroe. Yet both of his inaugural addresses contained references to how fortunate the nation had been to enjoy God's favor and how much the President hoped that favor will be continued.

Monroe died on July 4, 1831, six years after leaving the White House and five years to the day after the deaths of Thomas Jefferson and John Adams. Monroe's successor, John Quincy Adams, wrote about him that no one had done more than Monroe to expand the limits of the United States and foster the security of the nation, "thus strengthening and consolidating the federative edifice of the country's Union, until he was entitled to say, like Augustus Caesar of his imperial city, that he had found her built of brick and left her constructed of marble."

John Quincy Adams

"Except the Lord keep the city, the watchman waketh but in vain." With this second part of Psalms 127:1, John Quincy Adams ended his Inaugural Address on March 4, 1825, asking the favor of God's "overruling providence." Then he stepped forward to take the oath of office. "The President-elect...", reported the Washington *National Intelligencer*, "placing himself on the right hand of the judges' table, received from the Chief Justice a volume of the laws of the United States, from which he read, in a loud and clear voice, the oath of office." [11] Thus, Adams became the first President in the nation's history not to swear the oath upon the Bible.

John Quincy Adams was, like his father, a regular and disciplined reader of the Bible, usually two chapters every morning. Furthermore, as the son of a President and a lifelong servant of all of his predecessors, Adams was well aware of custom and precedent in the taking of the oath. He was known, though, by his contemporaries to be unmanageable, a somewhat derisive way of saying that Adams loved the nation more than a political party and cherished the individual liberty to think for himself. To use the Bible, might, in his mind, needlessly blur the separation of church and state so dear to the hearts of the early leaders. To use a book of laws would reinforce the principle of the rule of law superseding the rule of men, prominent in the political culture since first articulated in the Fundamental Orders of Connecticut in the 1630s.

Adams began his public service in 1781 at the age of fourteen as the private secretary to the American minister to Russia. He died in 1848 while still in public service as a member of Congress from Massachusetts, literally collapsing on the floor of the House and expiring in the Speaker's room. In between, Adams held more appointive and elective offices than any other President. He enjoyed success in every one, except the Presidency.

Author Glenn Kittler has noted that Adams' inauguration featured three *firsts*. President-elect Adams rode to the Capitol with Monroe, the first to be escorted by the sitting President to the ceremonies. Adams wore a full-length pants suit instead of the breeches fashionable theretofore. And, one of Adams' predecessors present at the ceremony was his father. [12] But it was a "second" which affected the inauguration of 1825 and helped to shape the largely unsuccessful administration to follow.

John Quincy Adams placed second to Andrew Jackson in the Electoral College. Neither earned a majority, though, and for the second time in 24 years, the House of Representatives was called upon to elect the President, each state having one vote. In dramatic fashion, the result depended upon one representative's vote deciding the direction of the New York state ballot. New York's choice would determine the winner of the election. Praying for divine guidance, so the story goes, the representative bowed his head and caught sight of a piece of paper on the floor. On the paper was written "Adams", and so the representative voted.

But Jackson's supporters saw something more sinister. One of the others receiving votes in the Electoral College was Henry Clay. When it was apparent that he would not emerge as the winner, Clay had campaigned vigorously to elect Adams, then was appointed Secretary of State. Jacksonians howled that a corrupt bargain had cost their man election, and for the next four years they thwarted much of what President Adams proposed to accomplish.

About Adams, one observer has written that he was "a man of reserved, cold, austere and forbidding manner. Though he could be charming and witty with intimates, he seemed to most people, including his admirers, "hard as a piece of granite and cold as a lump of ice." [13] Another wrote, "often high-principled in action to the point of rigidity, brusque in his speech to the point of incivility, righteous in manner to the point of sanctimony, John Quincy Adams was the model of the New England puritan - a man whose conscience, character and intellect could at times seem overbearing to those of lesser endowments." [14] Yet, there was the capacity for humility, most noticeable on Inauguration Day when he acknowledged that he came to office "less possessed of your confidence in advance than any of my predecessors." And he did not view service in the House of Representatives following his Presidency to be demeaning. "No person could be degraded by serving the people as a Representative to Congress," he told supporters in his district when they asked him to run. "Nor in my opinion would an ex-President of the United States be degraded by serving as a selectman of his town, if elected thereto by the people." [15] Adams is the only President to date to have served in Congress after his presidency.

Unitarian by affiliation, John Quincy Adams fiercely protected the political rights of the individual as articulated in the First Amendment. When pro-slavery forces in Congress succeeded in passing the Gag Rule, which effectively suppressed debate about slavery for many years, Congressman Adams annually proposed a bill to rescind it. He lost regularly for 13 years but finally prevailed in 1844. Freedom required watchfulness. For John Quincy Adams, the fact that the well-being of "the city" ultimately rested with the Lord was clear. But awake watchmen, even those "hard as granite and cold as ice," helped.

Andrew Jackson

Inaugurations generally bring celebration and gaiety to Washington D.C. and to the individual taking office. When the seventh President came to power on March 4, 1829, celebrations did, indeed erupt. Andrew Jackson represented an altogether different class of citizen assuming the Presidency, and for that there was great joy among the winners. Jackson, though, needed all of the courage and strength he could muster that day because his wife of 37 years, Rachel, had died in December, 1828, perhaps a victim of the viciousness of the campaign. Jackson had lost "the pilot in pious woman's form, who showed him the way to gain victory over self." [16] With little animation and speaking quite softly, Jackson delivered a relatively short speech before Chief Justice Marshall read the oath of office. Jackson repeated the oath, then picked up the Bible from the table behind Marshall, kissed it and bowed to the crowd. From that point in the day until the President literally escaped through a window at the White House to go to dinner, well-wishers mobbed him. One easily pictures the new President in something of a daze, wanting the company of Rachel all the while.

That Andrew Jackson attracted such adulation was not surprising. Victory over the British at New Orleans in the War of 1812 and his conquests in the Seminole Indian War made him the pre-eminent military hero of his age. His image was helped along by the fact that he had been born in a log cabin, away from Virginia or New England, and was viewed as a common man. Every predecessor was either a patrician

Adams or a well-educated Virginian who had played some role in founding the nation.

Jackson's reputation was enhanced by tales of divine favor. One priest claimed in 1816 that Christ sat on the right hand of God, Jackson on the left. Another story tells of an assassin who fired at Jackson twice from close range. Both times the gun jammed, a highly improbable occurrence. Surely, thought Jackson partisans, his good fortune must come from God. One historian described the American people as seeing in Jackson their hope for the nation, lowly born and self-made, heroic in deed, above all self-reliant. Why not protected by God as well?

Such a figure might find submission to divine authority through participation in a church difficult. Indeed, Jackson was not a religious man prior to or during his Presidency. He followed form, of course, in his Inaugural Addresses, ending the first with an expression of "firm reliance on the goodness of that power whose providence mercifully protected our national infancy..." His second inaugural address, however, concluded with a request for more direct political intervention by God. Under the threat of civil war, President Jackson had pressured the state of South Carolina to rescind its Ordinance of Nullification, asserting its power to ignore Federal laws with which it did not agree. To force compliance, Jackson was ready to use the army. Thus, he ended his speech in 1833 by saying: "Finally, it is my most fervent prayer to that Almighty Being before whom I now stand, and who has kept us in His hands from the infancy of the Republic to the present day, that He will so overrule all my intentions and actions and inspire the hearts of my fellow-citizens that we may be preserved from dangers of all kinds and continue forever a united and happy people."

Contemporaries would see Jackson's successes as evidence of God's blessing. Much as Puritan America believed wealth in the 17th century to be a sign of divine favor, so Jackson's supporters saw his achievements as symbolic. And his achievements were impressive. Trained in the law, though not at any school, Jackson had served in the House, the Senate and as a Justice of the Tennessee Supreme Court by the time of his 32nd birthday. His victory at New Orleans came over troops which had previously defeated Napoleon in Europe and spurred wild celebrations across the nation. Ironically, not known to the celebrants was the fact that the battle occurred after a truce had been reached between Great Britain and the U.S.

Following the defeat of the Seminoles in Florida, Jackson became Governor of that Territory for a year and then served once more in the U.S. Senate from 1823-25. The presidential election of 1824 illustrated his popularity, though he ultimately lost the election in the House of Representatives to Adams. Then came the bittersweet election of 1828.

Before Rachel married Jackson in 1791, she had been married to Captain Lewis Robards, but assumed herself divorced. She was mistaken, believing that a legislative permission for divorce obtained by Robards ended the marriage. In 1792, Robards did, indeed sue for divorce citing his wife's infidelity with Jackson. The Jacksons remarried when the divorce became final but the seed for political mudslinging was planted.

The Adams forces in 1828 resurrected the old stories, charging that a wild man from the West who flaunted the law by marrying a bigamous woman could not be trusted with power. Upon reading these accounts in the newspapers, Rachel suffered a heart attack in October 1828 and died two months later. Andrew Jackson blamed John Quincy Adams. As a result, like his father before him, Adams did not participate in the inauguration of his successor.

Jackson's Presidency produced several dramatic events: his veto of the National Bank, ending a point of political compromise which had lasted since 1792; the removal of Cherokee and other Native American tribes from their rightful lands in the Southeast to Oklahoma Territory; and a showdown with the South in the tariff nullification crisis which presaged the Civil War. By 1832, President Jackson's political opponents could find enough bold action asserting the prerogative of the President to brand him King Andrew in the campaign. But the people still loved him and he won a landslide. As rowdy as had been his first inauguration owing to the enthusiasm of the people, his second was orderly and dignified. His threat to fight South Carolina, made in his address, worked; a few days later their legislature did repeal the nullification ordinance.

At the end of his presidency, Jackson, or *Old Hickory*, returned to The Hermitage, his home in Nashville, Tennessee. There he joined the local Presbyterian Church. That act attracted extraordinary attention. The man of the people, conqueror of the conquerors of Napoleon, the "man of iron will," had submitted to the authority of God, proclaimed those to whom it mattered. So widespread was the interest that Currier and Ives, which printed several lithographs of Jackson's death bed, produced one in which the President's right hand rests on an open Bible as he breathes his last. And to what might the Bible have been opened? Perhaps Philippians 4:13 which aptly blends the power of God with the agency of man. "I can do all things through Christ which strengtheneth me."

Martin Van Buren

A ndrew Jackson hand-picked the Democratic nominee for President in 1836, Martin Van Buren, his vice-president, and a man Jackson regarded as a son. They shared more than politics; both bore the death of a beloved wife. Van Buren's Hannah, mother of their four sons, died in February, 1819. Van Buren chose to deal with his grief by losing himself in the other love of his life, politics. Effective at political organizing and credited by many for constructing the national Democratic Party in the 1820s, Van Buren reached the top on March 4, 1837 when he was sworn in as President.

Van Buren's political skills earned him the nickname *The Little Magician* and his magic seemed evident on that March day. The day was one of beautiful weather amid a succession of wet, cold ones. Nearly 20,000 people, including delegations of Native American chiefs in full dress, crowded around the platform on the east side of the Capitol to hear Van Buren's address. It was a half hour of details about the ways he would continue President Jackson's policies. He closed with a prayer for "the gracious protection of the Divine Being" and faced the new Chief Justice, appointed by Jackson, Roger B. Taney. Van Buren placed his hand on the family Bible, repeated the oath and, to the cheers of the crowd, kissed the Scriptures.

President Van Buren grew up in a strongly Dutch Reformed Church family in upstate New York. As an adult, he and his family were regulars at church, when he was home. His law career and political organizing activities kept him in Albany and New York City quite often. His presence at church was always noticeable; a great love of singing led him to sing more loudly than all others at services. His singing might have been the only way in which Van Buren did not blend. A fellow New Yorker said of him when he went to Washington to serve President Jackson, " Within 48 hours Van Buren will know everybody's opinion, but nobody will know his." [17] He was amiable with noticeable good manners and a fine command of himself. That ability to get along greatly aided him in his political career.

Van Buren's first political office came to him in 1808; he moved in rapid succession through the State Senate, State Attorney General, U.S. Senate, governorship, U.S. State Department Secretary, Minister to England and Vice President. Along the way, he established a reputation for love of the Union, moral courage and unheroic government. Public money, in his view, was for public purposes only. Yet he developed the party in New York through an effective spoils system, rewarding political support with government jobs, and he carried that technique with him to Washington. In his words and deeds, President Van Buren demonstrated his belief that the Constitution should be interpreted narrowly. For example, he spoke out strongly in support of strict separation of church and state and was firmly against a national bank. However, when it came to the powers of the President, he could see things differently. Van Buren carried out his predecessor's wishes, in defiance of the Supreme Court, by forcibly removing the Cherokee Nation from their tribal lands in Georgia and Tennessee.

Little distinguished President Van Buren's administration. Shortly after the inauguration, a financial panic struck and a long depression followed. The President promoted a plan for keeping the nation's money in government treasuries instead of commercial banks, but the scheme had the effect of slowing the circulation of money, a common malady in times of depressions, exacerbating the problem. Consequently, Van Buren lost the 1840 election to the newly emerging Whig Party and never again achieved significant political prominence, though he sought the presidential nomination twice more. The magic was gone for *The Little Magician*.

Van Buren lived to be 80, 21 years after leaving the White House. Many years before, he had carved on his mother's tombstone:

"Earth has an overcoming power,
It triumphs in the dying hour,
Christ is our life, our joy, our hope,
Nor can we sink with such a prop."

At Van Buren's funeral, there was no music save the singing of the hymn, "O God Our Help In Ages Past," a simple declaration of faith in the constancy of God, the prop provided by belief in Christ. Martin Van Buren gave his political party lifelong service and held that personal integrity and unheroic government were what the political leader owed to his followers. In another time and following some President other than a legend, Van Buren's steadfast commitment to duty might have been more noticeable. Still, there is much to be said for political leaders who place the ideals of public trust and honesty at the forefront of their political conduct. Martin Van Buren was such a man.

William Henry Harrison

"I deem the present occasion sufficiently important and solemn to justify me in expressing to my fellow-citizens a profound reverence for the Christian religion and a thorough conviction that sound morals, religious liberty, and a just sense of religious responsibility are essentially connected with all true and lasting happiness; and to that good Being who has blessed us by the gifts of civil and religious freedom, who watched over and prospered the labors of our fathers and has hitherto preserved to us insitutions far exceeding in excellence those of any other people, let us unite in fervently commending every interest of our beloved country in all future time."

William Henry Harrison delivered this too-long, florid sentence one hour and forty-four minutes into the longest inaugural speech in our history. One month later, he lay dead of pneumonia, the genesis of which developed on March 4, 1841, when Harrison insisted on delivering the speech in an icy wind without a hat or overcoat. *Old Tippacanoe* was 68. Braving the elements for the celebration provided him with a chance to show that he would be physically up to the job. Sad irony that he pledged not to run for a second term, as well.

The election of 1840 has become known as the first modern election because both candidates were nominated by party conventions and both parties engaged in sloganeering. *Tippacanoe and Tyler, too* began an American tradition to reduce candidates and/or issues to a few catch-phrases. Additionally, the election illustrated how opportunity in politics often follows luck; being in the right place at the right time.

Without doubt, Harrison was every bit the military hero his Whig
supporters made him out to be. But, his heroism was past history,
ending with the War of 1812. Following his military career, Harrison
served in the House for three years and the Senate for four before
becoming Ambassador to Colombia for a year. Anti-Masonics
nominated him for President in 1836, but otherwise nothing in his
career suggested that he would make a good President, and at 68 he was
retired anyway.

Still, because his opponent, Martin Van Buren, got painted as a rich
aristocrat for buying a new set of White House tableware with his own
money, and because the Whigs managed to construct Harrison's origins
as humble and common, the ex-general won 80% of the electoral vote.
In terms of political experience, President Harrison's running mate,
John Tyler, an ex-Jacksonian Democrat from Tennessee who broke
with Old Hickory to become a Whig, was better qualified. So were party
elders Henry Clay and Daniel Webster. However, Harrison's relative
clean political record (in doing little he had offended very few) and
military exploits combined with shrewd political handling to produce
the nomination and election. A very modern election, indeed!

The President-elect arrived in Washington for his inauguration on
February 10 by train, the first incoming Chief Executive to do so. He
spent the next three weeks meeting officials and making speeches. His
Whig sponsors celebrated heartily for this was their first time to win the
big prize. In between engagements, Harrison drafted his speech, asking
the most renown of his party's speakers, Daniel Webster, for help.
Webster labored in vain to make the speech shorter and less
pretentious. Though Webster once lamented that "in the last twelve
hours I have killed seventeen Roman proconsuls...dead as smelts, every
one," the final version retained many of the allusions to ancient times.
[18] Most agree that the essential message of the speech was clear:
whatever Congress wanted was fine with Harrison.

The nation in 1841 faced many problems, including a depression
and border disputes with several nations but the new President had a
distinguished Cabinet of Whigs led by Webster to assist him. So, in spite
of misgivings about his political skills or even his personal stamina,
optimism reigned as Chief Justice Taney administered the oath of office
to Harrison, as he became the ninth President of the United States.
According to custom, President Harrison kissed the Bible following the

oath. He then mounted his horse, rather than taking a carriage, for the ride to the White House.

He rode to the shortest term of office in our presidential history. He rode to become the first President to die in office. He rode to become the object of ridicule, for vanity and futility. There is no record of the Bible having been open for President Harrison's swearing in, but if it had been, to a point near the center, Psalms 119 might have been showing. The Psalmist might have reduced the message of this, the longest chapter of the Bible (176 verses) by saying "Blessed are the undefiled in the way, who walk in the law of the Lord." If, in similar fashion, Harrison had limited his testimonial to Christianity on that freezing Inauguration Day to "Let all know that I am a Christian. May God bless America," history might have turned out differently for William Henry Harrison.

John Tyler

As William Henry Harrison lay dying, Vice President John Tyler was at his home in Williamsburg, Virginia, completely unaware of the President's condition. Tyler had gone to Virginia because the Senate was not in session and the organization of the Harrison administration was being done by the Whig Party leaders who meant to control the President. Harrison died early Sunday morning, April 5; Tyler arrived in Washington on April 6.

Coming to office as he did, President Tyler was sure to set important precedents as the first to succeed a deceased incumbent. Tyler faced the additional problem of being a former Democrat; Whigs didn't trust him and had nominated him only to balance the Northerner Harrison with a Virginian. Whereas Harrison seemed to party leaders to be easily manipulated, Tyler possessed substantial political experience, and had developed deep and specific political preferences. Tyler's tenuous position in the Whig Party and the unprecedented situation of a dead President created the first showdown between Tyler and Whig leaders. In the process Tyler made his first significant contribution in behalf of the Presidency. On April 6, Congressional Whigs visited the Vice President in Washington and proposed calling Tyler "Vice President of the United States, Acting President." The Vice President noted that the Constitution did not mention an acting president and insisted on assuming the presidency with all the power and authority that entailed.

Next, the Whig leaders argued that Tyler needed to wait until the Chief Justice, Mr. Taney, returned to town before the oath could be taken. Tyler did not wait. He called for the Chief Justice of the U.S. Circuit Court for the District of Columbia, William Cranch, and took the oath at 12:00 noon on April 6 at the hotel where he was staying. In fact, few other Vice Presidents elevated to the presidency have actually been sworn in by a Supreme Court justice; any judge has sufficed.

Shortly thereafter, President Tyler called a Cabinet meeting where Whigs informed him that decisions were made by the majority, the President having one vote. President Tyler respectfully informed the Cabinet that he valued their opinions but that the authority to make decisions was his alone. Thus, within the space of a few days, John Tyler established several precedents relating to the power and prerogatives of an ascending Vice President.

Such political skill is not surprising in Tyler. Graduated from the College of William and Mary at age 17, Tyler won his first term in Congress at age 26. From that point on, Tyler occupied some political office until he left the Presidency in 1845 at age 55. Even then, there was one more term of service for Tyler (and one more precedent) when, at age 71, he began a two year term as a member of the Confederate Congress. He was, after all, a Virginian and, like General Robert E. Lee, endured great personal turmoil over the conflict between his state and his country. But, ever the states' rights advocate, Tyler sided with the South until his death in 1862.

Nicknamed *Honest John*, Tyler established a record as an independent politician. On such matters as the Missouri Compromise and tariffs, Tyler had voted like a Democrat. Yet, on other matters he was an ardent Jackson opponent. His various political offices included the Virginia legislature and governorship, Congress and the U.S. Senate, and he earned great respect for his discharge of each office. While President, he torpedoed his own Administration by telling Henry Clay, the Congressional leader of his own party, to stay at his end of Pennsylvania Avenue. In addition, he vetoed a bill to recharter the Bank of the United States, just as Jackson had done. The veto caused all of his Cabinet, save Daniel Webster, Secretary of State, to resign. Once Webster finished his work on a treaty with Canada establishing the nation's northern boundary, he quit, too. About the only accomplishment of note in the Tyler Presidency, aside from the

Webster-Ashburton Treaty of 1843, was the annexation of Texas in 1845, and that occurred after the election of 1844, just before James K. Polk became President.

Just as Tyler fiercely believed states rights to be the best guarantor of personal liberty, so his religious views celebrated the individual. Tyler officially belonged to the Episcopal Church, but he was more a deist, like Thomas Jefferson. He shared Jefferson's passion for the separation of church and state, and in his tolerant attitude toward Roman Catholics, demonstrated his belief that the freedom to believe as one wanted, guaranteed by the First Amendment, was an absolute in America. In his view, God created heaven and earth and the natural law which governed them. Man's obligation was to live a moral life in harmony with natural law.

Tyler's mechanistic view of the world allowed him to see slavery not as a religious issue but as an historical fact. The duty of any man was to live honestly and morally as best he could in whatever his condition. To him, the solution to the slavery issue was the African Colonization Movement, a stance quite like that of President James Monroe (next to whom Tyler is buried).

The life, political career and especially the Presidency of John Tyler serve as a symbol of the status of the nation. A man of integrity, politically seasoned and independent of mind, he stood not quite in either major political party. Becoming President by chance, he established precedents for the presidency which consolidated the strength of that national office. Yet, when the great split occurred in 1861, he joined in the governance of the rebels. Because the post-war 14th Amendment specifically disenfranchised those political officials of the South who had held office or commissions in the North, Tyler's death prevented the awkwardness of so punishing a former president. No one in the North officially acknowledged his passing, however.

"No man can serve two Masters," said Christ (Matthew 6:24) in the Sermon on the Mount. In the end John Tyler chose a side, perhaps not despising the other as Jesus suggested would happen, but surely with sadness. Upon becoming our tenth President, Tyler had said, "The institutions under which we live, my countrymen, secure each person the perfect enjoyment of all his rights." Tyler recognized, however, the dangers inherent in trying to live according to principle. "The purest and best of men have been neglected and abused. Aristides was banished and Socrates was poisoned. We should rather rely upon ourselves, and howsoever the world may deal with us, we shall, by having secured our own innocence and virtue, learn to be happy and contented even in poverty and obscurity." [19] Writing that in 1832, he echoed the message of the Beatitudes. In spite of significant actions in 1841 to preserve the office of the President, Tyler, indeed, found obscurity in the end. Such were the poisonous effects of disunion.

James K. Polk

Amidst the drenching rain on March 4, 1845, Chief Justice Roger B. Taney of Maryland moved forward on the platform on the east Capitol steps to administer the oath of office to James K. Polk of Tennessee. At 50, Polk was the youngest man to that date to become President. Though he had held both national and state office before, Polk had endured a campaign during which his opponents interrupted his rallies by chanting "Who is James K. Polk?" Once Polk swore the oath and kissed the Bible, the Marine Corps band played "Hail to the Chief" for him. All now knew who was James K. Polk, the eleventh President of the United States.

Perhaps Polk's hand, for the oath, should have rested upon Deuteronomy 34. There the Lord took Moses "unto the mountain of Nebo, to the top of Pisgah" to view the Promised Land. Then Moses died. President Polk added more than one million square miles to the territory of the United States during his four years. Then he left office and died within three months.

Indeed, Polk owed his Presidency to his belief that it was, as a New York editor wrote in 1845, "America's manifest destiny to overspread and to possess the whole of the continent which Providence has given us for the development of the great experiment of liberty and federated self-government entrusted to us." [20] In Polk's view, "to enlarge its limits (the Union) is to extend the dominions of peace over additional territories and increasing millions."

A former governor of Tennessee and twice Speaker of the House of Representatives in Washington, Polk was nonetheless a little-regarded candidate for the Democratic nomination. Then the previous Democratic President, Martin Van Buren, disavowed the annexation of Texas, thereby offending Andrew Jackson, the senior citizen of the Democrats. Jackson then threw his support behind Polk, a fellow Tennessean, a loyal follower who had earned the nickname *Young Hickory*. Polk's supporters went to the Democratic convention to deadlock it, looking to cause the party to turn to Jackson's preference. They succeeded, and Polk, the "dark horse" candidate, was nominated.

President Polk came to office resolved to accomplish four goals: restore the Independent Treasury system which held all of the government's money apart from any banks; reduce the tariff; establish the U.S. as the sole power in Oregon (power that had been shared with Great Britain); and acquire Texas and California. While Texas was annexed the day before he took office, the other goals Polk achieved. Then true to his word, he did not seek re-election in 1848.

Such clear articulation of political goals followed by achievement of those goals would seemingly endear a politician to his constituents. Polk even engineered a war which the U.S. won convincingly. But, President Polk did not win the "bounce" in popularity expected when a war is won, making any chance of re-nomination and re-election unlikely.

Even his standing in the minds of historians is mixed. Some see him as the only effective President between Jackson and Lincoln and praise his obvious achievements. Others see him as cunning and duplicitous, creating a war where diplomacy might have worked, then nearly causing the war to be lost in the early days by delaying his support for key generals because they were Whigs. His decision not to run for office again, made before his nomination in 1844, has been judged by critics as simply a way to buy the support of other more well-known party leaders who coveted the office themselves.

Indeed, President Polk's method of "extending the dominion of peace over additional territories" was war. Mexico had opposed the annexation of Texas and claimed its northern boundary to be the Nueces River. The U.S. regarded the Rio Grande River, some distance south, as the border. The President sent troops to the Rio Grande in April, 1846 expecting the Mexican Army to attack. They did.

Polk asked for a declaration of war, passed by Congress on May 13. Northerners had little taste for the war and anti-slavery forces viewed the war as an effort to win additional territory for slaveholders. The President's state of origin made his motives further suspect. Quickly, the war with Mexico became known as "Mr. Polk's War."

The President boasted that the war would last 60 to 90 days. The U.S. did win the war with relative ease but it did not conclude until September, 1847 when American troops entered Mexico City. By virtue of the Treaty of Guadelupe Hidalgo, the U.S. purchased the American Southwest (Arizona, New Mexico, Colorado, Utah, Nevada and California) and ended the war. It did not take long, however, for the issue of slavery to becloud this significant accomplishment, and Polk left office with his own party divided over his administration's achievements.

All this controversy lay in the future on Inauguration Day, however. President Polk's wife, Sarah, pious and proud of it, disapproved of drinking, dancing and cardplaying, and banned these activities from the White House. Her preferences shaped the inaugural activities as well. The Inaugural Balls did not include much revelry or dancing until after the Polks had made their appearances and returned to the White House early, to the great relief of many. This kind of puritanical seriousness characterized the President as well; he was known to work 18 hour days and seldom smiled. Such austerity matched well the contemporary outlook of the Methodist Church to which the Polks belonged for their entire married life.

In his Inaugural Address, President Polk spoke frequently about duty and, to the consternation of Democrats, about being "not...the President of a party only but of the whole people of the United States." Though a slave-owner and defender of states' rights, he flatly rejected the notion of secession and believed wholeheartedly in the Constitution. Noting in his address his relative youth as President, Polk observed that even "the more aged and experienced men who have filled the office of President...distrusted their ability to discharge the duties of that exalted station." Polk then said, "In assuming responsibilities so vast I fervently invoke the aid of that Almighty Ruler of the Universe in whose hands are the destinies of nations and of men to guard this Heaven-favored land against the mischiefs which without His guidance might arise from an unwise public policy."

Keeper of promises or unscrupulous politician? Self-righteously pious or humble servant of God's will for the geographical expansion of the United States? There is about James K. Polk something of an Old Testament patriarch, duty-bound to God and the people who follow him, engulfed in the vision of a promised land, destined not to enter it himself.

Zachary Taylor

General Zachary Taylor, the "hero of Buena Vista" to millions of Americans, stood before Chief Justice Taney on March 5, 1849 to take the oath of office as the twelfth President. Taylor's hand rested on the Bible that George Washington had used at his first inauguration. Finished with the oath, Taylor kissed the Bible and became the first regular Army career officer to be Commander-in-Chief of the United States. Taylor idolized Washington and was, indeed, the last U.S. President to have a personal memory of the first President's time in office The last to be born in the eighteenth century, Taylor was the first to become President with absolutely no previous political office in his background.

Not everyone close to Taylor cheered his victory. Margaret Taylor, his wife, let him know in the fall of 1848 that she prayed every day for him to lose the election. She wanted no part of the Washington D.C. social scene, and she feared that the Presidency might kill her husband. Cholera morbus did that, only sixteen months after Taylor assumed office.

Like career officers to follow him, Taylor had not clearly defined his political party preferences to others. In fact, he had never voted before 1848. His success in the Mexican War, though, made him a formidable candidate for either side. When first asked by the Whigs, he declined but said that he would accede to the wishes of his fellow citizens if they so inclined. The Whig convention nominated him on the fourth ballot.

In his campaign and in the first lines of his Inaugural Address, he sounded like a Whig. Fellow Whigs were not sure, however, what to make of his statement that he would be devoted to the "welfare of the whole country, and not to the support of any particular section or merely local interest." Did that mean he did not intend to support his own southern slavery interests, or would he abandon the predominant free-soil Whig position? In addition, Taylor declared that "honesty, capacity and fidelity" would be "indispensable prerequisites to the bestowal of office." To Whigs more interested in the political appointments which were the spoils of victory, such talk was worrisome.

What that talk demonstrated was Taylor's independence of mind. He was born in Virginia, raised in Kentucky and lived his adult life, when not on military assignment, in Louisiana. In short, Zachary Taylor was a product of the South. A southern Whig was unusual because so many Whigs opposed slavery, and Taylor owned slaves on his Baton Rouge plantation. Aware that some southerners already were talking about nullification or secession over slavery, Taylor warned that he would "personally lead an army against the South and hang any person guilty of rebellion." No President had been quite as blunt about the use of force internally since Jackson, another ex-general.

With little formal education, Taylor had nonetheless earned a lieutenant's commission in 1808, with some help from his cousin, Secretary of State James Madison. Gallantry in the War of 1812 established his reputation, and success in the Seminole War (1835-42) won him the nickname *Old Rough and Ready*. In 1846, Taylor's army won Mexican War victories at Palo Alto, Matamoros and Monterey. In the latter, however, he allowed the Mexicans to withdraw rather than surrender. This angered President Polk who transferred half of Taylor's army to another offensive, leaving Taylor undermanned at Buena Vista. The Mexican leader, Santa Anna, attacked in February 1847 with superior numbers. Taylor won, forcing Santa Anna to return to Mexico City and cementing Taylor's own popularity at home.

The fact that his wife smoked a corncob pipe as she accompanied him from battlefield to battlefield only enhanced Taylor's popular image. But she didn't want to go to Washington. She traveled there after the President-elect had arrived, in order to avoid the crowds, and she did not attend either the Inauguration ceremony or the Ball.

In a quirk of the calendar and custom, when President Taylor took office there had been no official and legal head of government for one day. March 4, 1849 was a Sunday; by custom, no Inauguration had occurred on Sunday. President Polk's term officially ended at noon on the 4th, and the official term of the President Pro Tempore of the Senate, the next in line, had expired on Saturday, March 3. His new term would begin when the new Senate convened on March 5 at noon. So President Taylor filled a vacuum.

Despite the lack of experience, President Taylor was an honest and determined leader. His stand on secession was the boldest until Lincoln's, and he advocated the quick admission of California in 1850 and New Mexico as soon as it was ready. In doing so, though, he showed his political naiveté.

To admit California would alter the free state/slave state balance and that worried the professional politicians, especially the Southerners. They denounced Taylor as a tool of the abolitionists, a silly charge given his own plantation slaves. But the national debate was ignited again, and it fell to Henry Clay, author of previous compromises in 1820 and 1833, to craft another.

President Taylor opposed the compromise, largely because he resented Clay, a fellow Whig, for not supporting Taylor's proposals concerning California and New Mexico. He threatened to veto the compromise. Then, following a July Fourth celebration at the Washington Monument, he fell ill. By July 9, President Taylor was dead.

Taylor had made a short speech on March 5, 1849, the shortest since his hero's, President Washington. He had concluded the speech by invoking the "goodness of Divine Providence," asking for "continuance of the same protecting care which has led us from small beginnings to the eminence we this day occupy." Such invocations were easy for Taylor, a lifelong Episcopalian, and entirely consistent with the sentiments of his predecessors. But Taylor went on to say that the United States would deserve that "continuance" only "by prudence and moderation in our own councils..." At the time of Taylor's death, bitterness and conflict ruled councils. Ironically, the territories he had helped to secure as a general provided new ground for the conflict he so ardently rejected as the solution to the debate.

"To everything there is a season," begins the third chapter of Ecclesiastes, "a time to be born, a time to die...a time for war and a time for peace." Zachary Taylor, the warrior, became President and sought peace. But the issues were growing too big for peaceful resolution and the Compromise of 1850 seemingly only delayed the time of war. Perhaps *old Rough and Ready* was lucky that his "time to die" came when it did.

Millard Fillmore

66 To you, Senators and Representatives of a nation in tears, I can say nothing which can alleviate the sorrow with which you are oppressed. I appeal to you to aid me, under the trying circumstances which surround me, in the discharge of the duties from which, however much I may be oppressed by them, I dare not shrink, and I rely upon Him who holds in His hands the destinies of nations to endow me with the requisite strength for the task and to avert our country from the evils apprehended from the heavy calamity which has befallen us."

Curiously, though the words were Fillmore's they were delivered by Speaker Howell Cobb. Fillmore had placed his hand on a Bible, taken the oath of office, administered by District Judge Cranch, on July 10, 1850, before a joint session of Congress, becoming the thirteenth President. He then left the House Camber, having asked Cobb to read his remarks.

The first words of the 245 comprising Fillmore's Inaugural Address praised the fallen leader, Zachary Taylor, as war hero and respected President. However, Fillmore, who was more presidential looking than the shorter Taylor, never really liked his predecessor and as President usually supported positions quite different than would have Taylor. Some of Fillmore's actions, like signing the Fugitive Slave Act to win approval for the whole Compromise of 1850, which would admit California to the Union, alienated him from his Whig Party colleagues. Such actions helped to explain his brief tenure in the national spotlight.

As a New York Whig, Fillmore had given regional balance to the ticket headed by the Louisianan pro-Unionist Taylor. Fillmore possessed impressive qualities, having begun his working career as an apprentice wool carder. Largely self-taught, Fillmore took up teaching school, all the while studying law. Admitted to the bar at 23, he won election to the New York State Assembly five years later and beginning in 1833, served five terms in Congress. In 1846, he began service as Chancellor of the University of Buffalo, a position which did not require regular attendance at the campus but was a major accomplishment for a man born in a log cabin in upstate New York. His political philosophy tended to be moderate, an inclination evident in his willingness as President to assist in the passage of the Compromise of 1850.

A charter member of the first Unitarian Society in Buffalo, Fillmore was a champion of reason over emotion. That attitude enabled him to view the Compromise with pragmatic dispassion. In his religious views, he was not terribly concerned about the existence of the Trinity except where the concept might tax reason. God, in his view, was benevolent and mankind virtuous. [21] Fillmore continued to be a lifelong supporter of his Unitarian Society even after his pastor criticized his political actions.

On the matter of church/state separation, Fillmore was clear. Several times in his career, he explained how, to him, the idea of justice could be separate from any dependence upon God. Early in his service to New York state, he was a vocal opponent of required religious oaths in court. Yet Fillmore readily took the oath of office as President on a Bible.

President Fillmore detested slavery. But, as he explained in a letter to Daniel Webster, slavery was an "existing evil and we must give it such protection as guaranteed by the Constitution." [22] The Constitution protected property rights as well, and slaves were regarded as property. Thus, he could sign the Fugitive Slave Act as a part of the Compromise.

Of course, the Compromise was intended as a way to relieve the pressure building in the nation over slavery. It did not. The intensity of feeling which deprived President Fillmore from even a faint chance at gaining the nomination for President for himself increasingly defined national politics. Eight years after Fillmore left office, the South seceded and war began. It was not the will of God for the country to "avert the evils" of the calamity of a nation split over slavery.

Though he made a futile stab at a political comeback in 1856 as the Presidential candidate of the American Party, a nativist party concerned about immigration, Fillmore spent the rest of his days practicing law and attending the Universalist Society meetings regularly. He lived long enough to see reason lose out to emotion in the form of civil war.

Franklin Pierce

Ninety minutes before inauguration time on March 4, 1853, the heavy snowfall stopped and the sun emerged. At 1:15 P.M., Franklin Pierce repeated "I do solemnly affirm" following Chief Justice Taney's lead, making the New Hampshire man the only President to affirm, not swear the oath. Normally, Pierce's hand would have rested on the Bible which he, as a active Presbyterian, read regularly. However, Pierce, believing himself to be sinful in the eyes of God, refrained from using the Bible.

The oath taken, the fourteenth President began his speech. Snow fell again, heavier than before, and the sky was dark, the wind icy. Far fewer than were present at the beginning heard the end of the speech. The new President must have worried that his luck would continue to be bad, and he was forced to worry alone. His wife had not yet joined him in Washington. If he had used the Bible, it should have been opened to Job 7: 20-21. "I have sinned; what shall I do unto Thee...And why dost thou not pardon my transgression...?"

Certainly, Jane Pierce, his wife, would have applauded such a choice. Religiously fanatic, Mrs. Pierce blamed a series of unfortunate events in their married life on the fact that God was punishing a sinful Franklin Pierce. Pierce had enjoyed a successful political career in the 1830s but developed a severe drinking habit as well. He had served two terms in the House of Representatives and won election to the Senate in 1836.

To save his marriage, though, Pierce resigned his Senate seat to return to Concord, New Hampshire to dry out and to practice law. Jane's view was that the Pierces had lost two infant sons because of Pierce's punishable iniquities, and the birth of a third son in 1841 gave them one last chance to please God. That could be done in New Hampshire but not in Washington D.C.

The Mexican War drew Pierce to enlist as a private although he soon won a commission as a brigadier general. His pro-slavery sentiments explained his willingness to join the war, and though wounded twice, he stayed on until the surrender. During the 1840s, he turned down offers to be the U.S. Attorney General, U.S. Senator and Governor of New Hampshire, so loyal was he to the promise he had made to Jane.

Little wonder, then, that few people ever seriously considered the possibility of Franklin Pierce as President. But his resolve to honor his promise wilted enough to allow New Hampshire delegates to place his name in nomination for President at the Democratic Convention in 1852. Thirty-three ballots occurred before he received any votes and sixteen more before he won.

When the news of his nomination came, Jane fainted. Pierce assured her that he had done nothing to encourage the nomination (a lie) and that he would do no campaigning (the truth). He said, however, that if the American people elected him, he had to serve. Thus, for the second time in four years, the wife of a candidate for President prayed for her husband to lose. To win, she believed, would be their personal doom.

Pierce won. On the way to Washington in January, the train carrying the Pierces crashed. The President-elect and his wife were not seriously injured. Their son died before their eyes.

Mrs. Pierce refused to proceed to Washington at that time. Not until March 4 neared did she begin the journey southward again. However, she learned about her husband's encouragement of the delegates to the Democratic Convention. When they met at her aunt's home in Baltimore on March 2, Jane announced to her husband that she would not be coming to the capital for the inauguration. Indeed, it was New Year's Day, 1854 before she was to make an official, though brief, appearance at a White House function.

On March 4, no Inaugural Balls occurred, ostensibly canceled due to the President's mourning his son. President Pierce managed to make clear his support of states' rights, slavery and the Compromise of 1850 in his Inaugural Address, speaking in the blizzard. But another cost was incurred. The wife of Pierce's predecessor, Abigail Fillmore, caught cold sitting on the platform during the ceremony and was dead shortly of pneumonia. Three weeks later, Vice President William King of Alabama died as well, though he had not been present on Inauguration Day.

Politically, President Pierce compiled a significant list of woes as well, confirming the judgment made of him by a New Hampshire neighbor: "Well, up here, where everybody knows Frank Pierce...he's a pretty considerable fellow...But come to spread him out over this whole country, I'm afraid he'll be dreadful thin in some places." [23] Though a supporter of the Compromise of 1850, he backed the Kansas-Nebraska Act of 1854 which undercut the Compromise. He enforced the Fugitive Slave Act which alienated Northern Democrats. He stood by, impotent, as pro- and anti-slavery forces shot each other in "bleeding Kansas." His representatives so oafishly tried to annex Cuba that the European powers forced Pierce publicly to disavow any aims for Cuba, a diplomatic disaster.

At least he had been a good steward of the public's money. When he left office, the government was in the black.

There was not much talk about renomination in 1856. No section of the Democratic Party supported him. Franklin Pierce returned to the privacy of life in New Hampshire to live out his last 12 years, enough time to witness war and the abolition of slavery. Pierce's personal tragedies abated but the national tragedy of civil war was to be played out.

Toward the end of his blizzard-marred address, President Pierce proclaimed that the nation would be ill-served if it rested its hope "upon man's wisdom." He continued, "It must be felt that there is no national security but in the nation's humble, acknowledged dependence upon God and His overruling providence." So, too, did Job acknowledge the omnipotence of God and submit himself to His grace and protection. Further travail followed but "the Lord blessed the latter end of Job more than his beginning." And the United States has survived to prosper as well.

James Buchanan

"No man can serve two masters," preached Jesus in the Sermon on the Mount (Matthew 6:24). As fifteenth President of the United States, James Buchanan was the last to try to govern a nation split to its spiritual core by the issue of slavery.

The usual gaiety surrounded Buchanan's inauguration on March 4, 1857. The new President's address brimmed with naive and unrealistic proclamations about how united were the United States, and a float in the parade featured a ship, representing the Union, and sailors running the flag up and down a pole, suggesting that the ship of state was well. A more accurate metaphor might have been the tree of Christ's sermon which brought forth fruit, but the tree was corrupt. Hence the fruit was evil. "Every tree that bringeth not forth good fruit is hewn down and cast into the fire." (Matthew 7:10)

Conflict over slavery had drawn blood even before Mr. Buchanan became President. In Kansas, where Congress had declared that the issue of whether or not the future state would have slavery would be decided by a vote of the people, supporters of both views rushed to the territory in an effort to pack it with like-minded voters. In some instances, settlers clashed with guns, earning the territory a reputation as "Bleeding Kansas." President Buchanan glossed over the conflict in his Inaugural Address claiming instead that popular sovereignty (letting the people vote) on slavery was the only true democratic way to decide the matter.

In the events leading to the moment Buchanan took the oath of office, one could find several ominous omens. The election results of 1856 provided Buchanan with a comfortable majority in the Electoral College, but the combined votes of the newly-formed Republican Party, specifically opposed to the spread of slavery, and the anti-slavery American Party, denied Buchanan a majority of the popular vote. Then, when the President-elect came to Washington to form a Cabinet, a mysterious ailment afflicted scores of people attending two different events in Buchanan's honor, killing several, including (eventually) his nephew and the Grand Marshal of the Inaugural Parade. Buchanan himself was seriously ill.

On Inauguration Day, President Pierce waited at one location for Buchanan to pick him up while the President-elect waited at another. Only when one man remembered seeing Pierce at the Willard Hotel did the presidential party come together and proceed to the Capitol, more than one-half hour late. Finally, well past one o'clock on this cold, clear day did Buchanan place his left hand on the Bible and repeat the oath, administered by Chief Justice Taney, the first swearing-in to be captured in a photograph. Ironically, within a year, Taney was to write a decision by the Supreme Court which effectively destroyed the compromises which had been made over slavery for the past 37 years. The opinion denied Dred Scott the status of person as well, decreeing him property without any right to sue. After that decision, the Civil War seemed inevitable.

To President Buchanan fell the fate of presiding over a dis-uniting nation. Triggered by the election of the Republican Lincoln in 1860, South Carolina first and then six others seceded from the Union before Buchanan's term expired.

How sad for Buchanan! At 65 the second oldest man to be elected to that time and our only bachelor President, Buchanan tried to follow the path of compromise which had kept the nation together for nearly 80 years in spite of the divisive, emotional issue of slavery. A well-respected man of Presbyterian upbringing and belief who spoke of the need to treat others, including other nations, with "Christian benevolence," James Buchanan had served the United States in various positions for forty years.

His first experience in government was a term in the Pennsylvania Legislature, 1815-1816. In 1821, Buchanan won election to Congress where he served for 10 years, coming to Washington just after the Missouri Compromise, the one specifically overturned by Taney. Following his first tenure outside the United States, as Minister to Russia, 1832-34, he returned to Washington for two terms as U.S. Senator from Pennsylvania. President Polk appointed him Secretary of State, and he was President Pierce's Minister to Great Britain, 1853-56. Some suggest that Buchanan was able to win the nomination and election in 1856 because he had been out of the country in the preceding years, marred as they were by turmoil over slavery.

Buchanan came to the presidency, then, with great experience in government. Perhaps he was the "tired old indecisive man" some historians judge him to be but, it is difficult to identify the actions he might have taken which would have averted eventual civil war. In the words of a famous Senatorial candidate in 1858, the house was divided against itself and Lincoln was right; it could not stand. Well-meaning, law-abiding citizens of the South, some prosperous, many not, believed intensely in their right as states to decide the issue of slavery. And they believed even more passionately that slavery was right. Some used scripture to buttress their beliefs.

Equally upstanding citizens elsewhere believed the institution of slavery to be immoral and the claim for state over national supremacy in political matters to be inconsistent with the Constitution. Bleeding Kansas, the raid by John Brown and his followers on an arsenal in Virginia for the purpose of arming the slaves, and the ascendancy of a political party pledged to limiting slavery only to those states where it already existed proved overwhelming hurdles to compromise.

Perhaps a Constitutional amendment reinstituting the old compromises or one guaranteeing the right to own slaves might have forestalled war. But the former was unattainable and the latter unthinkable. The South felt the need to defend its principles and the structure of its society. Northerners served a different master.

In his Inaugural Address, President Buchanan said, "I feel an humble confidence that the kind of Providence which inspired our fathers with wisdom to frame the most perfect form of government and union ever devised by man will not suffer it to perish until it shall have been peacefully instrumental by its example in the extension of civil and religious liberty throughout the world." Perish it did not nor was peace preserved. The corrupt tree of a society built upon slavery bore the evil fruit of war. Before there was to be a re-United States, there was to be the fire of war.

Abraham Lincoln

"None shall be weary nor stumble among them...whose arrows are sharp and all their bows bent, their horses' hoofs shall be counted like flint, and their wheels like a whirlwind." These words from Isaiah 5: 27-28, which lay beneath the hand of Abraham Lincoln as he swore the oath of office for a second time on March 4, 1865 come at the end of the prophet's vision of God's judgment upon sins in a chapter called "The Sevenfold Woe". The scripture is intended as reassurance to those who continue in the way of the Lord.

Moments before taking the oath, President Lincoln had spoken of woe, quoting Jesus in Matthew: "Woe unto the world because of offences! for it must needs that offences come, but woe to that man by whom the offence cometh!" (Matthew 18:7) Four years into the Civil War, after hundreds of thousands of deaths and injuries, his own side wracked with dissension over how to administer the impending cessation of hostilities, President Lincoln must have suffered greatly under the woes of war. In his speech, he noted, "Both (sides) read the same Bible and pray to the same God, and each invokes His aid against the other. It may seem strange that any man should dare to ask a just God's assistance in wringing their bread from the sweat of another man's brow, but let us judge not, that we be not judged. The prayers of both could not be answered. That of neither has been answered fully." Few have stated the tragedy of the Civil War more plainly.

Generations of American children have grown up learning the stories of Lincoln's life for he is one of our national legends. The myth of the humble, log cabin origins created for William Henry Harrison's campaign were true for Lincoln, and the sixteenth President was self-educated as well. Other parts of the legend---early life poverty, rail splitting, loser of more elections than he won (except for the state legislature)---are also fact. Little in his life before 1860 suggested that he would become the focal point whose election triggered secession and the war which followed.

Even after coming to office in 1861, President Lincoln faced hurdles which made the prosecution of the war to preserve the Union that much more difficult; incompetent or timid generals; a divisive peace movement in 1864 which nearly unseated him; members of his own party bent on retribution toward the South rather than reconciliation. He was neither legend nor hero in his lifetime, except to hundreds of thousands of slaves who regarded him as the Great Emancipator.

Certainly, there was nothing heroic about the start of his Presidency. His trip out of Illinois toward Washington featured a carpetbag full of grenades on the train and an attempt to derail the train in Indiana. Despite large and enthusiastic receptions in most of the major cities of the North, Lincoln ultimately entered Washington in secret under the cover of a deception planned by Pinkerton detectives to avoid an assassination attempt in Baltimore. For the inauguration itself, rifle squads took over rooftops and the Washington police made their presence obvious among the crowd in the Capitol Mall.

As the moment arrived for the presidential party to proceed from the Senate chambers to the outdoor inaugural platform, all hesitated as though no one wanted to be the first to go outside. Finally, Lincoln's principal opponent in the election of 1860, Senator Stephen Douglas, stepped forward and the ceremony proceeded.

At that first Inauguration Day, Lincoln took the oath of office from Chief Justice Taney, the southerner whose decision in the Dred Scott case of 1857 helped to fuel the passions for the war. Already, seven states had seceded, but Lincoln spoke in conciliatory words, rejecting the idea that the North would force slavery from the South and pleading for negotiations rather than war. He validated the rights of states to do much and firmly pledged to preserve the Union, arguing that any one secession could lead to all choosing to draw apart. As Lincoln spoke, Matthew Brady took his photograph; as he swore the oath, Brady shot again. Photos of the ceremony were now standard. After taking the oath and kissing the Bible, Lincoln and former President Buchanan left quickly. Shortly thereafter, Buchanan took his leave, telling Lincoln how happy he was to be out of office. Within five weeks, the Civil War had begun.

In the middle of the war, President Lincoln delivered arguably the most famous speech in American history at Gettysburg. The speech has the cadence, dignity and depth of scripture. Historian Gary Wills, in fact, notes implicit references to the Gospel of Luke in the address.[24] Such reference to the Bible, either implicitly or overtly, was common for Lincoln. Those who knew him well knew that he did not subscribe to the Christianity of any established church. He was more like the Transcendentalists of our own national tradition than anything else.

Yet his knowledge of the texts of the scriptures was extensive and his appeals to the Almighty for blessing and guidance came from a lifetime of belief. Small wonder, then, that the President's expressions of woe and the consequences thereof should be articulated in 1865 in the form of scripture.

President Lincoln's last (and best-known) words of the Second Inaugural Address blend the many themes of his life and Presidency; union, reconciliation, resolve and peace, all under the guidance of God. "With malice toward none, with charity for all, with firmness in the right as God gives us to see the right, let us strive on to finish the work we are in, to bind up the nation's wounds, to care for him who shall have borne the battle, and for his widow and his orphan, to do all which may achieve and cherish a just and lasting peace among ourselves and with all nations." "The work we are in;" was that work only the war? Or was it also the binding of wounds?

Though the war was essentially over by March 4, the work had not yet ended. Lincoln made more pointed reference to that fact when, just before his famous closing, he warned "if God wills that it (the scourge of war) continue...until every drop of blood drawn by the lash shall be paid for by another drawn with the sword" and concluded, using Psalms 19:9. "The judgments of the Lord are true and righteous altogether."

At that second inauguration, a man broke through police lines and almost reached the President before being apprehended. The man was questioned, admonished and then released. His name was John Wilkes Booth. Five weeks later, one week after the end of the Civil War, Booth reached the President with a gun and ended the woes of Abraham Lincoln.

Andrew Johnson

At 11:00 A.M. on April 15, 1865, Andrew Johnson placed his hand on the open Bible and swore the oath of office, Chief Justice Salmon P. Chase presiding. Johnson was succeeding the first American President to be murdered in office, though sadly not the last. A man believed by admirers to be the savior of the Union and of the Constitution lay dead, followed in office by another who had no formal schooling. Andrew Johnson had been trained and employed as a tailor before he entered politics. Now he was President.

Chief Justice Chase took note of where Johnson's lips touched when he kissed the Bible: "But as for them whose heart walketh after the heart of their detestable things, I will recompense their way upon their own heads saith the Lord God," read Ezekiel 11:21. In simple terms, the prophet was warning Israel that those who do evil can expect retribution. The Radical Republicans, President Johnson's bitter foes, could not have stated their intention for reconstructing the South more vividly than did Ezekiel. The Republicans were bent on punishing the South for the sin of secession.

Following the oath, the new President made a poorly thought-out speech in which he failed to mention either Lincoln or whether or not he intended to follow Lincoln's policies. Johnson concluded the speech: "Duties have been mine, consequences are God's." Sadly, Johnson's Presidency was no better than his speech.

The most significant support for that judgment lies in the fact that he remains the only President ever to have been impeached and tried, avoiding conviction by only one vote in the Senate. Yet even when faced with such dire consequences, President Johnson rejected the idea of offering political positions to the friends of Senators about to vote on the conviction, believing such politicking to constitute bribery. Johnson's integrity remained intact. The impeachment crippled his Presidency but he earned a measure of vindication when Tennessee returned him to Washington in 1875 as a U.S. Senator.

Although a Southern Democrat, Andrew Johnson was committed to the Union and, eventually, to freedom for slaves, two unpopular positions in the South in the 1860s. Those convictions earned him the Vice-Presidential nomination on a National Union ticket with Lincoln in 1864. As a politician, beginning as Mayor and proceeding through the House, Senate and the Governor's chair in Tennessee, Johnson had demonstrated his independent thinking. For example, he believed that a relatively few Southern slaveholders were foisting secessionist ideas on the majority of Southerners who were yeoman farmers not owning slaves. He voted against secession and remained in the U.S. Senate even after Tennessee seceded, moves which earned him threats on his life and physical beatings. But he was unmoved in his beliefs.

By 1863, Union forces had taken central and western Tennessee. President Lincoln appointed Johnson military governor and, within a year, Johnson had persuaded the legislature to rescind the vote for secession and abolish slavery in the state. A Jacksonian Democrat most of his political career, Johnson's decisive actions made him a natural selection as Lincoln's Vice President as the latter tried to re-stitch the fabric of union.

President Johnson took pride in the trade he knew and in tradesmen generally. At a meeting of mechanics in 1843, Johnson boasted, "Adam, the Father of the race, was a tailor by trade, for he sewed fig leaves together for aprons. Tubal Cain was an artificer in brass and iron; Joseph, the husband of Mary, the mother of Jesus, was a carpenter by trade, and the probability is strong that our Savior himself followed the same." [25] Such willingness to remember his roots earned him much respect with those who were not highly educated, at least until his pro-Union stance brought him overriding enmity in his home section.

Biblical allusion was common for Johnson in his political speeches although one, in which he described democracy as "a ladder, corresponding in politics to the one spiritual which Jacob saw his vision," brought him some derision when he delivered it as Governor in 1853. Reared as a Baptist, Johnson belonged to no church and once described his creed as "the doctrines of the Bible, as taught and preached by Jesus Christ." [26] He read the Bible regularly and was very attached to a fine English edition, with clear, large type, which he carried with him on his travels.

Yet when he came to the Presidency, so convinced were some that Johnson was an atheist that Congress considered the following resolution as a response to him: "Congress shall be opened with sincere prayer to the Giver of all Good for His blessing, and that the same should be done upon the terms laid down in the Gospel of Jesus Christ..." [27] The resolution was voted down but the tone of relations between the Republican Congress and the Southern Democrat (no matter his Unionist thinking!) was firmly established.

Never mind that Johnson's idea of how to re-unite the Union was much closer to Lincoln's than was that of the Congressional Republicans. Of course, Johnson's willingness to run for office with Lincoln had alienated him from his own party as well. President Johnson and the Radical Republicans in Congress made the congressional elections of 1866 into a showdown over Reconstruction. The choices were Lincoln's reconciliation versus the Republicans' retribution foretold by Ezekiel. President Johnson lost badly, and when he attempted to assert the power of the President over his own Cabinet by firing his Secretary of War, he was impeached. His crime was violation of the Tenure of Office Act, passed by Congress specifically to thwart President Johnson, a law ultimately ruled unconstitutional by the Supreme Court in 1926.

In another time and circumstance, such a blatantly political act as the impeachment and trial might not have occurred. But President Johnson had no strong political base and the wounds of war were scarcely covered over. In a sense, Johnson's presidency became another casualty of the Civil War. His strong commitment to principle and his unwillingness to bend or back down, laudable character traits, only exacerbated the conflict over how to treat the South. For one who had held political office almost continuously since 1830, President Johnson was surprisingly uncompromising, and he paid the political price for that.

In the end, Andrew Johnson won the opportunity to defend his reconstruction position as a U.S. Senator, though for only five months. He died in July, 1875, the reputation of his presidency permanently bleak. One imagines Johnson dying content, though, that his commitment to principle, personal and political courage and integrity never failed him, much like the Old Testament prophet upon whose words the first Johnson presidency was sworn to office.

Ulysses S. Grant

On Thursday, March 4, 1869, General Ulysses S. Grant took the oath of office to become the eighteenth President of the United States. His left hand was resting on "the Gospels," according to the account in the *New York Times*. Incredible as it may seem to 20th century observers, the account of the ceremony appeared *on page three*, not on the front page. For the fourth time in the eighty year history of the United States, the voters elected a victorious general to become the Chief Executive. Unlike those military men who preceded and followed, General Grant did not resign his army commission to become President, believing his presidential oath to supersede the other. Still, in a technical sense, Grant stands out as an exception to the accepted practice.

Clearly, Grant became President because of his success in the Civil War. He had no previous political experience, a deficit which manifested itself in his dismal, corruption-blighted years as President. A graduate of West Point, Grant had actually left the Army to farm and deal, with limited success, in real estate until the Civil War broke out. Early successes in the war campaigns in the West led President Lincoln, upset over timid and ineffective generalship in Virginia, to appoint Grant to head the Army of the Potomac. To General Grant had fallen the honor of accepting the surrender of General Robert E. Lee and his Confederate forces at Appomattox (Va.) Courthouse in 1865.

General Grant had the opportunity to enter politics earlier. President Johnson wanted the general to be his Secretary of War, but Grant had refused. In 1868, both political parties expressed interest in nominating Grant, though he was known to be a Democrat. But, his refusal of the Cabinet position endeared him to the Republicans and they succeeded in nominating him for President. Grant won 73% of the Electoral College vote.

After kissing the Bible on that first inaugural day, President Grant delivered a relatively short speech in a such low voice that few heard him. Among pledges to pursue the 15th Amendment and treat Native Americans more equitably, the President articulated a consistent theme in presidential addresses, that of divine blessing, but with a new twist. Predicting growing prosperity for the nation (a short term mistake given the depression which began in 1873 and ran for six years), President Grant suggested the source of the coming wealth. "Why, it looks as though Providence has bestowed upon us a strong box in the precious metals locked up in the sterile mountains of the far West and which we are now forging the key to unlock..." Certainly, in the previous 20 years, Americans had just begun to appreciate, through the many discoveries of gold and silver, the extent to which the nation was blessed with valuable natural resources. The President's prediction was correct in the long run. The land did provide riches born of God's creation which transformed the nation.

While the remaining states of the Confederacy adopted the 14th Amendment and rejoined the Union during the President's first term, little else positive happened. Instead, the history was decidedly negative, sullied by scandals involving members of his Cabinet, Congress and possibly even the Vice President. Nevertheless, President Grant won renomination easily although his Vice President, Schuyler Colfax, did not. With Senator Henry Wilson of Massachusetts as his running mate, Grant took 81% of the Electoral College vote. The voters evidently did not regard the President as accountable for the actions of his appointees, and, indeed, there was no evidence of the President being anything more than a bad judge of character.

President Grant understood that he owed his election in 1868 to his great popularity from the Civil War. His win in 1872 he attributed to the people's judgment of him as President. Consequently, he valued his re-election more dearly, viewing it as vindication.

March 4, 1873 was the coldest Inauguration Day on record (until 1981), temperatures well below 20 degrees, cadets and midshipmen present for the ceremony had not been prepared by their superiors for such weather and wore only light uniforms. Several lost consciousness during their more than 90 minutes in the cold. Still, the inauguration proceeded and the re-elected Grant took the oath a second time from Chief Justice Salmon P. Chase. On this occasion, the Bible was opened by the clerk at random.

In 1869, as the President completed his address, his daughter, Nellie, had run to hold her father's hand for the last few sentences, a touching display which was warmly received by the crowd. No such touches, planned or otherwise, warmed the crowd in 1873. The President, predictably, set out to defend his reputation in his address. He pledged pursuit of civil service laws and, again, more favorable treatment for Native Americans. He proclaimed the rebel states "happily rehabilitated," an exercise in wishful thinking.

Then the President proceeded to address the issue of the U.S. acquiring new territories. The one of immediate issue in 1873 was Santo Domingo. The President explained that he had no qualms about expansion because "...Commerce, education and rapid transit of thought and matter by telegraph and steam..." were developments binding together areas of the hemisphere and, indeed, the world. "...I believe that our Great Maker is preparing the world, in His own good time, to become one nation, speaking one language...when armies and navies will no longer be required."

None would doubt that President Grant foresaw that language as English and that nation as an American-style democracy. The lifelong Methodist was announcing the nation's missionary cause in the world. Inventions, expanding exploitation of natural resources like oil and the confidence gained by the nation by surviving a civil war would be powerful evidence of divine blessing to a President seeking to defend his administration. In doing so, Grant elaborated upon the long-term self-image of the nation. The City on a Hill would become the basis of one world, under God, and we would be active in promoting our ways to the nations.

More scandals marred President Grant's second term and the collapse of a major bank in 1873 led to a financial panic. Several years of a deep economic depression followed. Grant achieved some successes, however, most notably restored civil rights for most Southerners and some advancement in civil service reforms. But historians regard the Grant Administration to be one of the least successful and Grant himself to be out of his league as the chief political leader of the country.

"Peace" had been the slogan of the first Grant campaign. The man who had made war ferociously, overpowering his foe with wave after wave of humanity, accepting high casualties in a successful effort to deplete the South of its men, sought to be remembered as a man of peace. Though peace is a message of the Gospels upon which Grant took his oath of office, President Grant is not regarded as a peacemaker. But, his vision of America in the world proved remarkably on target.

Rutherford B. Hayes

Psalms 118: 12-13 reads: "They compassed me about like bees; they are quenched as the fire of thorns; for in the name of the Lord I will destroy them. Thou hast thrust sore at me that I might fall: but the Lord helped me." Sounds like fightin' words!

Rutherford B. Hayes was an unlikely warrior in the mostly hotly contested presidential election in the history of the United States. In 1876, Hayes was a compromise nominee of the Republican Party which was attempting to clear the blemishes on its reputation created by the corruption in the Grant Administration. He was a safe choice, having served honorably in the Union Army and in the House of Representatives before being elected to three consecutive terms as Governor of Ohio. Honesty was his chief political asset.

His wife, Lucy, was publicly perceived to be equally upright and moral. The first First Lady to hold a college degree, "Lemonade Lucy" was a staunch member of the Women's Christian Temperance Union. Strong Methodists, together the Hayeses sponsored a morning worship service after breakfast every day while they were in the White House. Sunday evenings, they invited other Washington officials to hymn services, and the Hayes were seldom alone at such gatherings.

Hayes' opponent in 1876 was Samuel J. Tilden, the Governor of New York. Tilden had made a reputation for himself as a reformer by breaking up Boss Tweed's control through his Tammany Hall political machine over New York City. Tilden, too, was highly regarded for his

personal and professional integrity. How ironic, then, that the election
of 1876 was the one most obviously tainted by fraud and corruption.

Though Governor Tilden won the popular vote by over 250,000
votes, the Electoral College was unable to select a winner. In four states,
Oregon, Louisiana, Florida and South Carolina, rival Republican and
Democratic slates of electors claimed to have won. The House of
Representatives could not reach a decision, either, and chose to appoint
an Electoral Commission to decide the issues, selecting seven
Republicans, seven Democrats and one independent. However, the
independent was unexpectedly elected to the U.S. Senate by his home
state, leaving a seven-seven split. Facing the March 4 inauguration date,
the Commission finally crafted "the Compromise of 1877" which
awarded the presidency to Hayes in exchange for several concessions to
southern states. Hayes was declared elected on March 2.
Understandably, feelings among Democrats ran high. They referred to
1876 as the year of the "Stolen Election."

Nevertheless, Hayes was the one to be inaugurated. Even then, there
was one more irregularity. March 4 fell on a Sunday. In the two
previous similar circumstances, the oath-taking was delayed until March
5. In 1877, fearful of any gap between the Grant and Hayes
Administrations, Hayes was sworn in Saturday night, March 3 by Chief
Justice Waite. Hayes took the oath in secret at the White House,
making him the only President to take the oath before the official
inauguration day (except for those succeeding deceased Presidents). For
two nights and a day, the U.S. had two Presidents.

March 5, under fair skies, Rutherford B. Hayes took the oath of
office in public to become the 19th President. At his request, the Bible
upon which he took his oath was open to Psalms 118: 12-13. Once
sworn, the new President delivered his speech. In it, like Lincoln, Hayes
began by restating the main points of his campaign, to reassure the
nation of his commitment to specific principles. Several times he
echoed former Presidents, notably Lincoln and Jefferson, as he sought
to establish his own legitimacy,

True to his word, one of his first actions was to remove all
remaining Federal troops from the South, allowing state and local
authorities to govern. Reconstruction was officially over. In the
remainder of his speech, the President tried to pump up the spirits of a
nation in the third year of economic depression and to address issues of

the hour; currency and civil service reform. He also floated the idea of a constitutional amendment limiting the President to a single, six-year term. His Administration made little progress on any of these fronts.

Hayes concluded with a plea for "general acquiescence" in the compromise which made him President. Few of his opponents were listening. Surely, in the days between November, 1876 and March, 1877, Hayes must have felt "compassed about like bees" with his political enemies "thrusting sore" at him "that he might fall." But, he didn't. The Hayes Administration, which began with the country in economic depression and ended with renewed prospects for prosperity, passed with little distinction and far less controversy than was presaged by the circumstances of his election.

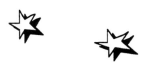

James A. Garfield

"And above all, upon our efforts to promote the welfare of this great people and their Government, I reverently invoke the support and blessings of Almighty God," concluded James A. Garfield in his Inaugural Address. Wrote the *New York Times* the next day, "The close of the address was most impressive, and as the strong man who had won a great political fight stood with hands uplifted appealing to God for aid in the trial before him, there was the utmost silence upon the stand and the plaza. When he had concluded his speech, the President-elect handed his manuscript to President Hayes and turned to the Chief Justice (Waite), who arose to qualify him for the high office upon which he was about to enter. That officer administered the oath. James Abrams Garfield bent low, kissed the Bible and was declared President of the United States." In headlines, the *Times* proclaimed this to be "the most memorable inauguration day ever known in Washington."

Sadly, dramatic descriptions of events have disappeared in modern times, even though the penchant for hyperbole ("the most memorable ever") has not. The man who swore "so help me God" on March 4, 1881 did not need excessive praise to make himself impressive. James A. Garfield didn't want to be President, and he worked through 33 ballots at the Republican Convention to dissuade the delegates from nominating him.

Yet he carried notable credentials. His public service prior to 1881 occurred in the House of Representatives; he remains the only Congressman ever to move directly to the Presidency. He was a former college president and professor of Latin and Greek at Hiram Institute, Ohio. Hiram was the college started by one of the frontier denominations in America, the Disciples of Christ, a brotherhood to which Garfield was committed. He brought intelligence, humility and the instincts of a consensus-builder to the U.S. Presidency. Tragically, he was shot less than four months after taking office, dying two months later.

Garfield grew up in Ohio without a father, who had died early in the President's life. He worked at a variety of jobs, like carpenter and boatman, to put himself through college, first at Hiram then at Williams College. He seemed destined to a scholarly life when the trustees elected Garfield, a devout member of the Disciples of Christ, to be president of the college. His prominence in Northern Ohio gave him a platform from which to condemn slavery. Small wonder, then, that he joined the Union forces in the Civil War, rising quickly to become a Brigadier General at age 30. Gallantry at Chickamauga earned him Major General rank.

Articulate and educated, decorated as brave and prominent, Garfield moved easily into elective politics. He began his service in Congress in 1863 and by 1880 was his party's leader. As such, he knew well the major issues of the day: civil service reform, currency, tariffs and reconciliation of the South to the Union. When the Republican Convention in 1880 split between "Stalwarts" who supported former President Grant and "Half-Breeds" who supported Senator James G. Blaine of Maine. Garfield emerged as the compromise candidate. Ironically, he had come to the convention as someone else's campaign manager.

A truncated Presidency invites speculation about what might have been. President Garfield came to office with great promise. Friend and foe alike found him to be principled and fair. As a Disciple, Garfield belonged to a group which believed passionately in the priesthood of all believers yet held clear views about morality and acceptable behavior. As a former abolitionist, Garfield also held deep feelings about what ought to be the lot of the men and women freed by the war in which he had performed so gallantly.

Garfield's Inaugural Address, which so captured the *Times* writer, offered clues to what he held most vital. He began with a lesson in American constitutional history, culminating in the Civil War. Then he addressed race. "So far as my authority can lawfully extend," he said, "they [the emancipated race] shall enjoy the full and equal protection of the Constitution and the laws." He went on to champion the power of the vote and the importance of the free exercise of that right by all citizens.

Then Garfield told his audience that illiteracy presented the greatest threat to the nation. He did not blame the South for the plight of the blacks, calling instead for a united effort by North and South to solve a national problem. Echoing Jefferson's call for an educated citizenry, Garfield proposed universal education of all children, black and white. He proclaimed education of "successors" as "high privilege and sacred duty" and closed his argument quoting Isaiah. "Let our people find a new meaning in the divine oracle which declared that 'a little child shall lead them,' for our own little children will soon control the destinies of the Republic."

Prosperity, the coinage of silver and the need for a civil service system to fill government jobs filled the remainder of his address. Tragically, it was a disappointed office-seeker, Charles J. Guiteau, who shot President Garfield on July 2, 1881. Guiteau blamed Garfield for the failure of many Stalwarts to win government appointment as the spoils of Republican victory. Garfield lingered for two months before dying in September.

In the full text of Isaiah 11:6, however, is a symbolic summary of the successes achieved by Garfield in his career and of the vision of true national reconciliation which died with him. "The wolf also shall dwell with the lamb, and the leopard shall lie down with the kid; and the calf and the young lion and the fatling together; and a little child shall lead them." Garfield, the teacher, saw the possibility of a reunion of the spirit of the nation and had a plan to achieve that. Guiteau denied President Garfield the chance to carry out the plan.

Chester Alan Arthur

On September 19, 1881, Vice President Chester Alan Arthur received a telegram from several Cabinet members attending President Garfield. The message warned Arthur that the President would die shortly. At 10:35 P.M., he did. Within an hour, Arthur held the telegram announcing Garfield's death in his hand as he sobbed uncontrollably, "like a child" in the words of his butler.[28] Chester Arthur considered himself unqualified to be President. After all, he was just a New York Republican machine politician fired for his misuse of patronage as the Collector of the Port of New York in 1878. Yet on a closed Bible in his own study in New York City, Arthur swore the oath administered by New York Supreme Court Justice John R. Brady and became the 21st President.

Arthur was an add-on, a ticket-balancer for Republicans in 1880, a Stalwart supporter who would bring New York's electoral vote to the Ohioan Garfield. Educated in the law, Arthur's service during the Civil War was as Quartermaster General of New York State. As a New York City attorney and active member of the Senator Roscoe Conkling political machine, Arthur developed a reputation mainly for "fine clothes and elegant living" as one observer put it. [29] If Arthur felt unfit to be President, many more soberly shared his view.

What most people expected was an administration dominated by machine politics, including graft, corruption and proliferating political patronage, the practice of rewarding party faithful with government jobs. What the nation got was an honest, hard-working President who repudiated his machine colleagues by rejecting legislation they favored. He even pushed the Pendleton Act of 1883, also known as the Civil Service Act which established merit as the basis for filling some government positions. Additionally, his Administration prosecuted members of his own party who were accused of defrauding the government. His political courage cost him the nomination of the Republicans in 1884, largely because the bosses were determined to get even.

The reformation of the reputation of President Arthur began even before Garfield's death. The *New York Times* praised his conduct as "self-effacing after a fashion as manly as it was statesmanlike. He never lost sight of the fact that he was merely the vice-president of the United States, watching like the rest of his fellow citizens over a life which he and they were sincerely anxious should be spared." Of course, the *Times* went on to castigate the Vice President's "unsavory friends."

Even though three previous Vice Presidents had succeeded to office upon the death of the incumbent President, there was no clearly established protocol for how to proceed. The Cabinet members with Garfield at his death believed that the Vice President should be sworn in soon after the President died; others felt that a more public ceremony in Washington was needed. Thus, Arthur took the oath twice, the second time on September 22 at Arthur's office in the Capitol. In an historical first, two former Presidents, Grant and Hayes, were witnesses.

The *Times* reported: "The Chief Justice (Waite) raised the Bible from the table, opened it and passed it to the President, who placed his hand upon the printed page. The Chief Justice then slowly administered the oath, with his eyes upon the face of the President, who kissed the book and responded, 'I will, so help me God.'" If the Bible had been opened to its midpoint, President Arthur's hand might have been over Psalm 121. "I will lift up mine eyes unto the hills, from whence cometh my help. The Lord is thy keeper...The Lord shall preserve thy going out and thy coming in from this time forth, and even for evermore." Given his tears in the night two days before, the reassurance of the Psalmist would have met Arthur's mood.

The new President declared that September 26 should be set aside for fasting, humiliation and prayer. "I earnestly recommend all the people to assemble on that day in their respective places of divine worship (for Arthur, an Episcopal Church), there to render alike their tribute of sorrowful submission to the will of the Almighty God and of reverence and love for the memory and character of our late Chief Magistrate."

In the next day's edition, the *Times* editorialized: "There are mysteries which we cannot penetrate, but we are better for devoutly asking for the blessings we crave and for accepting with humble submission the afflictions that we are meted out by a wisdom and love whose purposes we cannot follow." Such thoughts rarely find expression in editorials of the 1990s, but were acceptable in that time and circumstance. What the author wrote about the death of Garfield fits the service of Chester Alan Arthur as President: "There are mysteries we cannot penetrate." President Arthur made sure, with the passage of civil service reform, that President Garfield's murder would precipitate a change in the country for the better.

Grover Cleveland

" And let us not trust to human effort alone, but humbly
acknowledging the power and goodness of Almighty God, who
presides over the destiny of nations, and who has at all times been
revealed in our country's history, let us invoke His aid and His blessings
upon our labors." After Grover Cleveland delivered these final words of
his Inaugural Address on March 4, 1885, he stepped toward Chief Justice
Waite to take the oath.

"A young man holding a small, morocco-covered, gilt-edged Bible
stood between the Chief Justice and Mr. Cleveland and presented the
book. It was a well-worn [small] volume, the gift of the mother of
Grover Cleveland." [30] This Bible had been a part of the desk for
every public office in which Cleveland, a devout Presbyterian, served.
Cleveland placed his right hand on the book and took the oath. Then,
after kissing it, he put the Bible into his coat pocket. He would have the
opportunity to use it again in just such a manner.

Grover Cleveland occupies a unique niche in American history; the
only person elected twice to non-consecutive terms. Serving as the
twenty-second President beginning in 1885, Cleveland lost the White
House in the election of 1888 but won again in 1892. When he
accompanied McKinley to the inaugural festivities of 1897 as the
retiring President, Cleveland became a further entry into the book of
anomalies associated with inaugurations; he was the first President to be
a participant in four consecutive transfers of power.

"Grover the Good," as he was called in 1884, came to Washington following service as Governor of the State of New York, Mayor of Buffalo and Sheriff of Erie County. The first Democrat elected since 1856, Cleveland's victory resulted from his carrying his home state of New York by just one thousand votes. Regarded as an honest man who had made his reputation by fighting the Tammany Hall political machine in New York, Cleveland's Democrats drew epithets from Republicans as the party of "Rum, Romanism and Rebellion," the latter an inelegant reference to the Civil War. Passions ran high. During the campaign, Cleveland received a number of personal threats. The concern for his physical safety was enough for him to arrange a special and secret arrival in Washington.

"The Reform President," trumpeted the *New York Times* in its March 5, 1885 headlines. One delegate to the convention nominating Cleveland had noted that "we love him for the enemies he has made." Cleveland's immediate predecessor, Chester A. Arthur, had taken up the cause of civil service reform and laid down the foundations of a merit-based federal work force. President Cleveland continued the work, placing a significant number of jobs which had previously been prizes of political patronage under civil service control.

Whether to expand the money supply through the free coinage of silver and deciding the appropriate level for America's protective tariffs were the other two major political issues of the decade. Defending a lower tariff than the Republican Party demanded led to Cleveland's loss in 1888 to Benjamin Harrison, the man he subsequently defeated in their 1892 rematch.

Another *Times* column in 1885 reported "Rejoicing Everywhere---Inauguration Salutes---Decorations and General Jollifications." Probably because of their twenty-four year absence from the White House, the Democrats conducted jubilant celebrations throughout Washington. The parade was so big, for example, that a last-minute adjustment, allowing Arthur and Cleveland to reach the Capitol for the ceremony, needed to be made. On his way back to the White House, the new President rode through a shower of rose petals. Yet for all its reputation as a party of party-goers, the Democrats pulled off an orderly ceremony, parade and inaugural ball for its new champion.

Upon completion of the oath in 1885, President Cleveland shook hands with the Chief Justice, then with the others on the platform. By

1893, there was one other person to acknowledge. Cleveland came to office for his first term a bachelor. Within a year, he had made Frances Folsom his wife. It was she to whom he turned first in 1893 following his handshake with Chief Justice Fuller to deliver a warm and triumphant kiss.

While March 4, 1885 had been sunny, "surpassing fair weather," sleet, snow and rain chilled the 1893 affair. [31] The weather presaged Cleveland's second term. A financial panic later in 1893 led to a severe economic depression which lasted most of Cleveland's second term. Significantly, however, when Cleveland left office in 1897, he enjoyed the respect of people in both parties for his honesty, independence and commitment to principle. Because of the depression, though, Cleveland was not even considered for the 1896 nomination of the Democratic Party.

As in 1885, Cleveland delivered his Inaugural Address from memory, talking, coincidentally enough, mainly about economic concerns. In his 1885 address, Cleveland had observed that "Your every voter, as surely as your Chief Magistrate, exercised a public trust." Cleveland won his second term campaigning against an incumbent associated with weak leadership, favoritism toward the privileged and corruption among high government officials. Cleveland took seriously the investment of the voters' trust in their President, and in the depression which plagued his second term, he took actions which were politically unpopular in pursuit of what he believed to be the good of the nation.

"Grover the Good" closed his 1893 address: "Above all, I know there is a Supreme Being who rules the affairs of men and whose goodness and mercy have always followed the American people; and I know he will not turn from us now if we humbly and reverently seek his powerful aid." The little Bible given to him by his mother was closed each time Grover Cleveland took the oath of office. But as much as for any of his fellow Presidents, the verses from Micah upon which Governor John Winthrop sought to establish his American "City on a Hill" would apply. Doing justice, loving mercy and walking humbly with God seemed second nature to the President to whom Americans gave a unique second chance.

Benjamin Harrison

"God has placed upon our heads a diadem and has laid at our feet power and wealth beyond definition and calculation. But we must not forget that we take these gifts upon the condition that justice and mercy shall hold the reins of power." So proclaimed Benjamin Harrison in his Inaugural Address. March 4, 1889 dawned a windy, rainy, dreary day, and the weather made Harrison inaudible more than ten feet away. The speech was too long anyway, especially given the circumstances. Harrison could well have used Micah 6:8 as his choice of scripture on which to be sworn, given the sentiment expressed in his speech. But the wet weather made an open Bible out of the question for the pious Mr. Harrison.

Benjamin Harrison's grandfather held the record for the shortest Presidency; one month. In some respects, the younger Harrison's effective Presidency was even shorter. Benjamin came to office, not on the strength of his own record of political service or significant electoral effort. Rather, Harrison won nomination as the candidate most governable by the party bosses.

The period between his election and his inauguration demonstrated how weak he was in comparison to the men responsible for his nomination. The *New York Times* editorialized that Harrison must be dissatisfied with some of the Cabinet appointments he felt forced to make. No doubt Harrison was able to spend a quiet weekend before inauguration because those wanting favor and office didn't bother to seek him out; they dealt directly with the bosses.

In the early days of his career, Benjamin Harrison did not seem such a passive participant in his own life. He passed the bar at 20, earned wide respect in his state of Indiana and when the Civil War erupted, served as a Brigadier General in the Union Army. Prior to his nomination in 1888, he had served one term as a U.S. Senator, though he had lost his bid for re-election in 1886.

Personally, President Harrison and his wife, Caroline, were cautious, abstemious, conservative, devout Presbyterians. Capital city stories depicted Harrison as afraid of the new electric lights in the White House. They did not drink or dance which led to some remarkably dull Inaugural Balls until the Harrisons went home. On the other hand, a daily ritual in the Harrison home was one-half hour of prayer and Bible reading, and they attended Presbyterian services on Sunday regularly.

Politically beholden to the Republican bosses, President Harrison supported the various trusts which had grown to dominate the corporate world. Ironically, the first significant anti-trust legislation in U.S. history, the Sherman Anti-Trust Act, passed during his term, but he did nothing to see the law enforced. A fan of high tariffs "to protect infant industries," President Harrison's tariff policies had the distinction of producing such a huge government revenue surplus that the Congress became known as the "Billion Dollar Congress." Diadems, power and wealth, indeed! There seemed little to connect President Harrison with the millions of common people for whom he had stated his desire for justice and mercy.

Yet, in the circumstances of his inauguration, there are evidences of his concern for others and his personal humility. The rainy weather led inauguration organizers to consider holding the ceremony indoors, in the Senate chambers. But the chamber offered only limited seating. Harrison understood that the inauguration was for all the people to see, not just the party elite. So, he resolved to hold the ceremony outdoors. A photograph of the ceremony shows the wisdom of the decision. In spite of the rain, thousands attended.

Most departed before Harrison had finished his speech, soaked and unable to hear him anyway. Therein lay a metaphor for his Presidency.

The *New York Times* described the actual oath-taking: "Chief Justice Fuller [in an overcoat rather than judicial robes] held in his hand the

Bible that General Harrison had brought to Washington to be sworn
upon. He preferred it to the new book that Clerk Nicolay has regularly
purchased for the occasion. It was the Harrison family Bible and it will
stay in the family as a valued souvenir...General Harrison, protected by
the umbrella of the Sergeant-at-Arms, removed his hat as he held the
book and then raised it to his lips."[32] The wind and rain were such
that only the act of kissing the Bible cued the crowd that the oath-
taking had ended, and then they cheered.

In his address, President Harrison uttered something of a prayer.
"Entering thus solemnly in covenant with each other, we may
reverently invoke and confidently expect the favor and help of
Almighty God--that He will give me wisdom, strength and fidelity, and
to our people a spirit of fraternity and a love of righteousness and
peace."

The voters abruptly broke that covenant in 1892 when they
returned Grover Cleveland to the Presidency in a landslide. Harrison,
dull and cold but honest, had been betrayed by widespread corruption
among many of the appointees imposed upon him by the bosses. Sadly,
the loss in 1892 came four months after the death of his wife.

Benjamin Harrison lived on for nine more years and actually
remarried in 1896. But the cloud of unfulfilled promise, sometimes
outright failure, which marked his post-Civil War career, is the
overwhelming judgment of history about his Presidency. Harrison
confidently expected the favor of Almighty God. But justice and mercy
could not take the reins of power from the bosses to whom Harrison
owed his political soul.

William Mckinley

66 The highway of the upright is to depart from evil: he that keepeth his way preserveth his soul. Pride goeth before destruction, and a haughty spirit before a fall." (Proverbs 16: 17-18) On March 4, 1901, upon taking the oath of office a second time, William McKinley kissed a Bible opened at random to Proverbs 16, a collection of "moral virtues and their contrary vices." Marshal McKenney, Clerk of the Supreme Court, noted that McKinley's lips seemed to touch the verse which reads "the wise in heart shall be called prudent." The accidental connection of moral virtues from the Bible and President McKinley seems providential. There was an air of a moral crusade to the McKinley Administration with the Chief Executive serving as Chief Priest.

Fiscal conservatism and the extension of U.S. power globally undergirded the McKinley philosophy. McKinley became the 25th President in the midst of a significant economic depression. Furthermore, Populism with its radical proposals for political and economic change, had flamed across the agrarian South and West. However, because this rural movement failed to unite effectively with urban labor, the banker/industrialist-led Republican Party secured the election of McKinley, the pro-business Governor of Ohio, to the Presidency.

McKinley came to office with considerable political experience. A Civil War veteran who had enlisted as a private and risen to the rank of major, McKinley studied law after the war and won his first political office in 1869 as a county prosecutor in Ohio. He had won a seat in Congress in 1876 and served a total of ten years between 1877 and 1891. Ohioans elected him governor in 1892. Throughout his political career, McKinley was loyal to manufacturing interests and left his mark in Congress as the author of the inordinately high McKinley Tariff of 1890.

High tariffs, the gold standard and the defense of major trusts, such as in sugar production, formed the Republican party's platform which President McKinley vigorously pursued. Supporting the sugar interests prompted particular attention to Cuba. That island, only ninety miles from Florida, was a possession of Spain and prime agricultural land for growing sugar cane. Stories about Spanish atrocities in Cuba gave the United States cause for advocating Cuban independence. When the US battleship, *Maine*, exploded in Havana's harbor, killing 260 Americans, the McKinley Administration had a pretext for taking Cuba away from Spain. The "splendid little war," (Secretary of State John Hays' description of the Spanish-American War) cemented U.S. presence in Cuba and produced Puerto Rico and the Philippines as prizes to the nation for winning. American sugar companies were winners, too.

At McKinley's first inauguration, the first to be filmed with motion pictures and called by the *New York Times* "a very impressive ceremony," the newly elected President took the oath with "the air of an advance agent for prosperity." Swearing his oath, administered by Chief Justice Fuller, on a large Bible presented by the Bishop of the Methodist Church in Africa, McKinley made clear in his address that he believed the United States to be the chosen people of God.

"I assume the arduous and responsible duties of President of the United States, relying on [the support of the people] and invoking the guidance of Almighty God. Our faith teaches us that there is no safer reliance than upon the God of our Fathers, who has so singularly favored the American people in every national trial, and who will not forsake us so long as we obey His commandments and walk humbly in His footsteps."

These comments in his 1897 inaugural address presaged a revelation McKinley felt he received with regard to the U.S. take-over of the Phillipines after the Spanish-American War. McKinley had to decide whether or not to allow the U.S. to become an empire, exercising administrative and political control in other places around the world. There was considerable opposition in the nation to the idea of the U.S. as an imperial power. But others, like Theodore Roosevelt and, ultimately, McKinley, championed Americanism as the ideal for all the world to emulate. Having outposts around the world clearly served the country's international trade interests and most accepted that reality. Actually administering whole territories was a different matter.

President McKinley argued that the Philippines could not be returned to Spain and were unready for self-government. During his regular period of prayer one evening, the President understood God to give the U.S. a mission "to educate the Filipinos, and to uplift and civilize and Christianize them, and by God's grace do the very best we could by them..." He then authorized the use of Spanish-American War veterans to quell a revolt by Filipinos who (already Christian under Spanish rule, but Catholic, not Methodist) did not see much difference between Spanish and American domination. Both were foreign rulers. McKinley, the devout Methodist, became McKinley, the crusading missionary.

A nation pleased by economic prosperity and newfound respect worldwide elected McKinley again in 1900, this time with Theodore Roosevelt, Governor of New York, as his running mate. Business interests looked forward to four more years of the White House in the hands of one favorably disposed toward their interests. To McKinley fell the honor of being the first President to be inaugurated in the 20th century. A popular President, a new century, prosperity and world power; what could spoil such a bright future?

Leon Czolgosz, an anarchist from Cleveland, could and did. Upset that President McKinley was so popular when he, Czolgosz, was not, the unemployed factory worker followed the President to the Buffalo Exposition on September 6, 1901 and shot him twice. McKinley lingered and even rallied a few days following the shooting. But by Friday, September 13, even McKinley realized that he was about to die, President McKinley passed away at 2:00 A.M. on September 14, the third President to be shot to death.

Succeeding him was Roosevelt whom McKinley had felt to be too liberal and too eccentric. New York Republicans worked hard to gain Roosevelt the Vice-Presidential nomination as a way of getting him out of New York and into political obscurity. Now, by virtue of an assassin's bullets, "that damned cowboy," to use a phrase of Republican leaders at the time, was President. McKinley's moral crusade ended, replaced by a Progressive's vision of America. As it happened, the new President might well have written those phrases in McKinley's Inaugural Address of 1897 which spoke to God's "so singularly" favoring the American people in every national trial. A President was dead, but as the nation was to see, the crusade would be continued.

Theodore Roosevelt

"For unto whomsoever much is given, of him shall much be required..." (Luke 12:48) Theodore Roosevelt lived his life believing that much had been given to him. Equally powerful was his belief that he had much to give back to the world. In deftly aligning his own will with the aims of the nation, Roosevelt the President came to symbolize his country in the first years of the twentieth century -- brash, expansive, opinionated on world affairs, with unlimited potential to become pre-eminent in the world. The Bully Pulpiteer, the first modern President, intended to deliver as leader what was required of himself and the nation.

Where President McKinley's style more resembled the well-meaning Methodist minister and missionary, Theodore Roosevelt approached life and politics with the passion and moxie of the pugilist he was in college. The mere fact of his being in position to become President on September 14, 1901, upon the death of McKinley, testifies to his irrepressible energy, boldness and ability to irritate even his supposed allies. Characteristically, Roosevelt was attending the yearly conference of the Fish and Game League when the President was shot and wounded in Buffalo, New York. Assured that McKinley would survive, TR went mountain-climbing. Megaphones and rifles were needed to gain his attention on the slopes of Mount Marcy when the news of McKinley's decline toward death came. Roosevelt arrived back in Buffalo too late to see McKinley, and in the afternoon of September

14, he took the oath of office from Federal District Judge John Hazel to become the 26th President.

President McKinley's main Republican sponsor, Mark Hanna, groaned shortly afterward, "Now look, that damned cowboy is President of the United States." Roosevelt was born and bred a New Yorker, but the cowboy image captured the bold, adventuresome, somewhat unpredictable quality of the new President's character. Sickly in childhood, he developed great physical prowess by such activities as boxing at Harvard, and actually spending time out west in the Dakotas running a ranch. A voracious reader, Roosevelt also wrote, churning out more than twenty published books in his lifetime. Born to the family of a machine Republican, he found his political allies among the progressive wing of the party, a faction which would inevitably clash with the Old Guard.

As Assistant Secretary of the Navy, 1897-98, Roosevelt had demonstrated his boldness (and his belief in the value of sea power) by ordering the U.S. Pacific Fleet to the mouth of Manila Bay. TR's boss was gone that afternoon and, acting as Secretary, Roosevelt judged that war with Spain was imminent. Therefore, the fleet needed to be ready to take the Philippines swiftly. Events unfolded as Roosevelt had wished.

Of course, a war offered Roosevelt the chance for personal involvement, as well. So, he organized the Rough Riders to fight in Cuba against the Spanish. Though the details of the battle have suffered embellishment from hero-makers, Roosevelt's forces prevailed in what became known as the Battle of San Juan Hill, and Colonel Roosevelt came back to New York as a war hero. Winning the governor's chair that fall of 1898 proved easy.

But the New York State Republican machine didn't need a governor who was so much his own man. Consequently, they plotted to send Roosevelt to political oblivion by winning for him a place on McKinley's ticket in 1900 as Vice President. Six weeks before his 43rd birthday, the Colonel-rancher-author-reformer was President. What an ideal stage for a crusader whose enemies were human weakness and corruption.

"Malefactors of great wealth," like trusts and coal companies that exploited miners, became early targets for President Roosevelt. Roosevelt, the conservationist, used the Reclamation Act of 1902 to set aside huge acreages for National Parks and other public uses.

Roosevelt, the tactician, supported Panamanian rebels as they seceded from Colombia, and won for his efforts the opportunity to build the Panama Canal. Roosevelt, the world leader, arranged for the U.S. to run the Philippines for the next forty years. During his first term, the Pacific cable made global communication by telephone possible and the Wrights flew the first airplane. President Roosevelt had nothing to do with the latter events directly, though he was our first President to fly. However, both of these technological achievements represent the enormous potential for great things which Roosevelt believed to be America's destiny, indeed its obligation.

Small surprise, then, that Roosevelt won 60% of the popular vote in 1904. March 4, 1905 was a great day for Roosevelt. He would, as he said, "come into office in my own right." Washington, D.C. overflowed with well-wishers including veterans from the Civil War and Roosevelt's own Rough Riders. Republican bosses might not have wanted him, but President Roosevelt was clearly the people's choice. The mere sight of the President approaching the rostrum for the ceremony created such cheers that only Roosevelt's taking charge of the proceedings by nodding to Chief Justice Melville Fuller could end them. For the parade awhile later, more than two hundred thousand people lined Pennsylvania Avenue, more than ever before at an inauguration.

Before the ceremony, Secretary of State John Hay, who had served President Lincoln in the White House, gave Roosevelt a ring, the crown of which contained a lock of Lincoln's hair from his deathbed. With that powerful connection to the last great Republican President on his finger, Roosevelt placed his hand on the Bible, recited the oath, finishing with "I swear, so help me God," and kissed the Bible. He then began his address, uncharacteristically short and without once using the word "I." "My fellow citizens, no people on earth have more cause to be thankful than ours, and this is said reverently, in no spirit of boastfulness in our own strength, but with gratitude to the Giver of Good who has blessed us with the conditions which have enabled us to achieve so large a measure of well-being and happiness."

Calling America "the heir of the ages," the President continued, "Much has been given us, and much will rightfully be expected from us." The rest of the address was a call to duty, accepting the obligations of our power at home and abroad. There could be no shrinking from the responsibility of being the city on a hill, a beacon unto the ages.

In his second term, and indeed in the rest of his life, Theodore Roosevelt sustained his pattern of forcefully asserting what he believed was right, always in opposition to human weakness and corruption. A photograph of his Inaugural Address in 1905 shows Roosevelt standing with his head tilted upward, strong and proud, his form unshielded by a lectern, the whole focus of the picture clearly the President. TR made the Presidency the focus of national attention in a way far more familiar to us today than to the Founding Fathers. Indeed, he called the position a "Bully Pulpit," a platform from which the President ought to chart the course and then steer the mass of followers to action. His talents were many and he set out to multiply their effects. In doing so, he transformed his nation's political scene and its position in the world. Could any more have been expected?

William Howard Taft

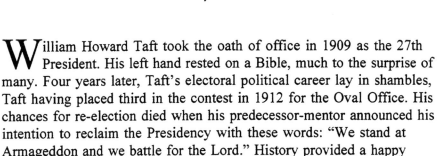

William Howard Taft took the oath of office in 1909 as the 27th President. His left hand rested on a Bible, much to the surprise of many. Four years later, Taft's electoral political career lay in shambles, Taft having placed third in the contest in 1912 for the Oval Office. His chances for re-election died when his predecessor-mentor announced his intention to reclaim the Presidency with these words: "We stand at Armageddon and we battle for the Lord." History provided a happy ending for Taft, however, because he died in 1930 as Chief Justice of the United States Supreme Court.

Taft was a Unitarian, believing in the concept of God as one person, not three as held by those believing in the Trinity. In the Unitarian tradition, no special profession of faith is required of members. Thoughtful consideration and discussion is preferred to doctrine. Not holding to a specific creed, Unitarian fellowships determine the policy of the community of believers by taking the time needed to discuss varying viewpoints. In the weeks following Taft's election in 1908, many people performed a remarkable leap of logic, circulating the rumor that Taft would not be able to swear on the Bible because he belonged to a church that didn't believe in Jesus.

Taft came to the Presidency by the grace of Theodore Roosevelt. By nature cautious and judicious, Taft's early career was as a lawyer and then a judge in his native Ohio. His first positions with the national government were also in the law, first Solicitor General, then Circuit

Court Judge. Just prior to his nomination and election as President, Taft served Roosevelt as Secretary of War where his amiability and thoughtful consideration of alternatives before actions served him well. When Roosevelt suggested to Taft that he succeed TR, Taft declined at first. He really wanted to be on the Supreme Court.

President Roosevelt persuaded Taft to run, thinking Taft to be a progressive like himself. Compared to some, President Taft was progressive. But, not compared to Roosevelt, as would be plainly evident during Taft's term of office.

In March 1909, though, the men were still allies. Roosevelt thought highly enough of his successor to invite him to move into the White House on March 3. On Inauguration Day, they had breakfast together and discussed what to do with the day's ceremonies since a blizzard had immobilized the city. Largely in deference to the age (76) and condition of Chief Justice Fuller, the President-elect agreed to take the oath in the Senate chamber, the first time that had happened since the second Jackson Administration.

Following an invocation by Senate chaplain, Edward Everett Hale, and a recitation of the Lord's Prayer, the new Vice President, James Sherman, spoke briefly. Then the Chief Justice and the President-elect moved onto the dais. Appropriately for this particular President, the Chief Justice held the Bible used to swear in justices of the Supreme Court for generations. Taft placed his left hand on the Bible, took the oath, and following the words, "so help me God," took the Bible in both hands and kissed it. In doing so, the new President had demonstrated reverence for tradition, if nothing else, and the act precipitated loud and extended applause.

President Taft's inaugural speech listed the ways in which he hoped to sustain the policies of his predecessor and the few new initiatives he might undertake. Roosevelt was especially pleased by the parts pledging continuity. No stirring oration, the address featured several minutes of focus on race relations. Ever full of faith in the law, President Taft noted the 13th, 14th, and 15th amendments as protections of the basic rights of "the Negro." He argued that Southern laws were beginning to come in line with the intent of the amendments, especially the 15th, guaranteeing the right to vote. History would prove him prematurely optimistic in such claims.

Then, remarkably, he explained that, while holding no racial prejudice himself, he could not appoint any Negroes to office. Doing so, he said, might "do more harm than good" by inciting those who were prejudiced. The President then concluded by invoking "the considerate sympathy and support of my fellow citizens and the aid of Almighty God."

President Taft's approach to race issues illustrated his general nature. His style and temperament did not include precipitous acts. The President enjoyed some successes during his Administration but none which called for dramatic or bold action. Taft sponsored the income-tax amendment, made significant changes in the federal service, including more jobs to be filled through civil service, acted as a good steward of the many reserves of natural resources owned by the nation and saw two states admitted, New Mexico and Arizona. But on other matters, especially with respect to his avid enforcement of the Sherman Anti-Trust Act, Taft disappointed the progressive followers of Roosevelt who had helped to elect in 1908. Where Roosevelt had sought merely to regulate trusts, Taft seemingly wanted to destroy them altogether. As a result, when Taft won re-nomination in 1912, Teddy Roosevelt's supporters bolted from the Republican Party, leaving Taft to represent the "old guard" at a time when the country was overwhelmingly progressive in orientation.

Taft left the Presidency to join the faculty of Yale Law School. Eight years later, President Harding appointed him Chief Justice; Taft thus became the only person in U.S. history to hold both high offices. One historian wrote about him. "He was a huge man. [And he was! He weighed over 300 pounds.] And the movement of his mind was as sedate as his walk." [33] Meeting with limited success as President, Taft was in his element on the high court. The Unitarian from Ohio was then in the job where discussion and thoughtful consideration were essentials of the job. He could speak only when ready and only on topics of his choice. Roosevelt's "Bully Pulpit" was best left to other men.

Woodrow Wilson

The League of Nations and Woodrow Wilson's Fourteen Points are excellent examples of America's desire to apply the rule of law to international affairs. How fitting, then, that when Woodrow Wilson bent to kiss the Bible following the oath of office in 1913, his lips touched the following words from Psalms 119: "So shall I keep thy law continuously for ever and ever." Ironically, the Bible had been opened at random.

Woodrow Wilson brought to the White House a unique personal background with regard to religion. Wilson's father, Thomas, was a Presbyterian minister, and no doubt Woodrow experienced the preacher's-kid pressure to follow in his father's footsteps. He didn't, choosing instead an academic career and developing a fine reputation as a scholar studying Congress and the Presidency. But his life reflected early lessons about obedience to God's laws, and in his political career, he manifested both the moral certitude and the inflexibility which often besets those too sworn to immutable law.

The major events of Wilson's Presidency unfolded like Crusades. Elected as a progressive Democrat, Wilson enjoyed a first term marked by many successes in his domestic crusade for social justice. The Federal Trade Commission, the Clayton Anti-Trust Act, the Federal Reserve Bank, the direct election of U.S. Senators and the progressive income tax extended the protection of the national government to guarantee individual citizens fairness in a sound economic system. In his Inaugural Address, reported the *New York Times*, Wilson included eleven epigrams which the newspaper said distilled Wilson's aspirations and beliefs. "The firm basis of government is justice, not pity" went one. Another was "we know our task to be no mere task of politics but a task which shall search us through and through." [34]

The crusade in behalf of democracy in the world consumed his second term. "The war to make the world safe for democracy," and "the war to end all wars," were applied to the First World War. That war concluded with a vain attempt at a peace free from retribution. The effort at such a peace consumed Wilson. In his attempt to sell participation in the League of Nations to the American people, he suffered a debilitating stroke, effectively ending his Presidency though he survived. No mere tasks of politics, the effort to enact a different kind of peace and to unite the nations in a world organization sought nothing less than the replacement of the historical reality of spoils going to the victor with an idealist's vision of reconciliation. Wilson preached "open agreements openly arrived at" to a world too accustomed to secrecy and self-interest.

All this lay ahead as Wilson stepped forward at 1:10 P.M. on a balmy day March 4, 1913 to take the oath of office. The Chief Justice, a soldier for the South in the Civil War, Edward D. White, led Wilson, a Virginian by birth, through the lines of the oath. Wilson's left hand rested on Psalms 119. The recitation completed, the twenty-eighth President delivered a short and characteristically idealistic speech.

That March 4, Wilson came to the White House as a successful reform Governor of New Jersey, following a happy tenure as President of Princeton University. Four years later, seasoned by the triumphs of domestic Progressivism, but troubled by too-frequent brushes with the war in Europe, Wilson swore the oath a second time. The Zimmermann note, proposing an alliance between Germany and Mexico in the event of U.S. entry into the war, had recently been discovered. American shipping, sailing under our interpretation of neutrality which clearly favored Britain, was constantly threatened by German U-boats. War for the United States seemed inevitable.

Wilson had defeated Charles Evans Hughes by a very small margin. A switch of 2,000 votes in California would have elected the Republican. Wilson's first wife, Ellen, died in 1914; a second Mrs. Wilson, Edith, would be witness to the private oath-taking in 1917. The ceremony occurred on a rainy Sunday, March 4, inside the President's office at the Capitol. This time the Bible was opened intentionally to the Psalms, to the 46th chapter. "God is our refuge and strength, a very present help in trouble," read the verse the President kissed.

The public re-enactment the next day was played to thirty-five thousand witnesses under sunny but windy and cold conditions. National Guard troops provided a greater level of precaution and protection than at any inauguration since Lincoln's. Such was the level of tension over the war and our impending entry. Chief Justice White read the oath, Wilson responded, "I swear, so help me God," and the President delivered an address as brief as his first one.

Wilson's Presidency presents the elements of tragedy. Certainly, the idea that law ought to govern the affairs of nations as well as men is noble, and the notion that peace treaties should not punish the loser but prepare the ground for new relationships devoid of war is a real-life application of the Beatitudes. But practical politics, in the international arena and at home, made the attainment of such lofty goals impossible. As the one who envisioned a world ruled by these principles, Wilson resisted much compromise. And compromise is essential in politics, the art of the possible. Ultimately, Wilson's idealism killed his Presidency.

The conclusion of the 1913 speech provided a fitting summary to Wilson's work as politician and President. "Men's hearts wait upon us; men's laws hang in the balance; men's hopes call upon us to say what we will do. Who shall live up to that great trust? Who dares fail to try? I summon all honest men, all patriotic, all forward-looking men to my side. God helping me, I shall not fail them, if they will but counsel and sustain me."

In the end, in his vainglorious attempt to transfer the rule of law from his nation to the world and to transform relations between nations, Wilson did fail. But, the United States was changed forever. After World War One, there was no doubt that the United States was the leader among nations, in both economic and military terms. The President of the United States could not dictate the peace in 1918-19, but the opinions of all Presidents following Wilson mattered greatly around the world.

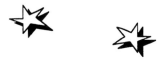

Warren G. Harding

"What doth the Lord require of thee, but to do justice, and love mercy, and to walk humbly with thy God." These words from the prophet, Micah (6:8), claimed so long before by Governor John Winthrop as the underlying philosophy of his city-on-a-hill society, lay beneath the hand of Warren G. Harding as he became the 29th President on March 4, 1921. The Bible on which he took the oath had a history, too; Washington had used it twice.

With such illustrious roots to the inauguration and with the President's popularity as a man of the people, Harding's administration began in an atmosphere of great hope. As was the case with several of his predecessors, Harding didn't so much seek the office as did party bosses seek a public figure who could win and be controlled by them. Harry Daugherty, Harding's campaign manager, invented a familiar phrase to American politics when he predicted prior to the convention Harding's nomination "at 2 a.m. in a smoke-filled room." Harding's principal asset was that he looked like a Roman Senator, appropriately Presidential.

The inauguration featured new practices as well. Harding and Wilson were the first incoming and outgoing presidents to ride in a motorized vehicle from the White House to the Capitol. Harding's address was the first to be amplified by a loudspeaker system. The President and Mrs. Harding declared their desire not to have much ceremony around the transition of power, perhaps because of concern for Wilson, perhaps because the Duchess, as Harding's wife became known, was not given to excessive displays.

And, Harding epitomized normalcy, a word not known to the world before he had used it in his campaign. He was a Baptist businessman from the heartland of the nation, reminiscent of President McKinley and the other prominent Midwestern politicians of the 19th century. Following the trauma of the First World War and facing the prospect of world leadership, there was in America in 1920 a widespread desire to retreat to earlier times, perceived to be safer because they were known. Wilson had been an intellectual and an idealist, persuaded of the correctness of his view of America's role in the world. Harding made no demands on the people for leadership in the world or greatness. That was the essence of normalcy.

Harding, Senator from Ohio at the time of his election, and publisher of the Marion *Star* before that, claimed no special brilliance as his own, either. Instead, he made plain his intention to surround himself with the best Republican minds he could find and let them run the country. A Cabinet featuring Herbert Hoover, Charles Evans Hughes and Andrew Mellon fulfilled one part of his promise. Unfortunately, Albert Fall, Jess Vaughn, and Harry Daugherty were also prominent in the Harding Administration. Their misdeeds, in Veterans Administration, Teapot Dome and Elk Hills scandals, contributed to the most corrupt administration since President Grant, imprinting an odor on the reputation of the Harding Presidency.

The nation needed a healer following the clamor of world war and the fight over the League of Nations, and President Harding was temperamentally right. He preferred compromise and conciliation to conflict, and excelled at the nostrums which calmed the nation as it turned inward, away from international responsibility. A good-hearted man, he probably rose one office too high in his career for his own well-being. Yet, in the early months of 1921, Harding seemed right for the job.

Most of the accomplishments of the Harding Administration are appropriately attributed to others; the creation of the Bureau of the Budget and consolidation of one Federal Budget annually, the Washington Naval Conference, the separate peace with Germany. Then, on a good will tour of the nation, Harding's term ended abruptly with his death in August, 1923 in San Francisco. There was little public accomplishment to temper the private shortcomings of the President - fathering children out of wedlock, drinking alcohol during Prohibition, incessant card games late into the night - creating for Harding the historical reputation of being one of the country's two worst Presidents.

There was much in Harding's pre-Presidential life to suggest that he really wanted to do justice, that he really did love mercy. In his campaign to return the U.S. to normalcy and a lower international profile, Harding seemed to be following the admonition from Micah about humility as well. Unfortunately, in the devious political activities of some of his associates, and in the adulterous actions of his own personal life, "with thy God" seems to have been forgotten.

Calvin Coolidge

"I have faith that God will direct the destinies of the nation." So said Calvin Coolidge in his official statement the day after Warren Harding died and Coolidge became President. "I think I can swing it," he is reported to have said, immediately after taking the oath.

Calvin Coolidge was the second Vice President in the 20th century to have an unscheduled swearing-in because of the death of his predecessor. That might have been the only bit of untidiness surrounding the terms of our thirtieth President. Laconic and shy, routinely working long hours to model good in government, Coolidge's passion for economy and efficiency matched the stereotype of the starched New England Yankee.

The setting for his taking the oath early in the morning of August 3, 1923 (preserved in a artist's drawing for the Boston *Post*) reflected Coolidge's character and the tenor of his administration to follow. The *New York Times* reported that "the taking of the oath was a simple and solemn scene." Administering the oath was Colonel John Coolidge, 78, "sturdy and active despite his years," a notary public of Windsor County, and the father of the new President.

In a room where the "furnishings were those of an ordinary New England farmhouse of the better class" stood a table on which lay a Bible which belonged to his mother. The Vice President raised his right hand and put his left on the Bible. Colonel Coolidge read the oath of office which he had found in a text in his library. "As the end was reached, President Coolidge ... said in a low, clear voice, ' I do, so help me God.' A moment later the group dissolved and President and Mrs. Coolidge retired." [35]

Coolidge succeeded a very popular President, as effusive and outgoing as Coolidge was reserved. Not known on the night of the transfer of power was the extent of corruption within the Harding administration. Coolidge's personal honesty and his thrifty stewardship of government enabled Republican candidates to be elected in 1924 and 1928 despite revelation about the scandals. Coolidge came to office with specific intentions about policy; favor business, limit government, stay out of other nations' affairs. In what might be the longest quote attributed to Coolidge, he praised the industrial engine of the nation thus: "He who builds a factory builds a temple. He who works there worships there."

Puritan virtue ran deep in Coolidge. Early in his life, Coolidge spent hours reading the Bible to his grandfather. The section he read first to him was one which remained a favorite throughout Coolidge's life, John 1. "In the beginning was the Word, and the Word was with God, and the Word was God. And the Word became flesh and dwelt among us." For the entirety of his career prior to becoming Vice President, as mayor of Boston, then as Governor of Massachusetts, Coolidge was equated with diligence, integrity and the idea that public office was a public trust.

With an apparent prosperity spread widely in the nation, except on farms, Coolidge won re-election easily, defeating John W. Davis, the Democrat, and Robert M. LaFollette, Progressive candidate, with 54% of the popular vote, and 72% of the electoral vote. Given the Harding scandals, these margins clearly indicated Coolidge's popularity with the people. Indeed, Coolidge was so excited, he went to the opera the night before his second inauguration.

Inauguration Day 1925 reflected similar understatement. Coolidge ordered simple ceremonies. Decorations in the city and along the route from the White House to the Capitol were sparse. To limit the crowds, few bleachers were erected. There was no inaugural ball. Political organizations, which might have provided some joyousness in the event, were banned from the parade which featured military units and small delegations from each state. The parade lasted only 55 minutes.

Coolidge took the oath for his first full term from Chief Justice William H. Taft, himself a former President. Once again, Coolidge's left hand rested on the Bible, the same one used in 1923. This time, the Bible was open to John 1.

Then Coolidge delivered his address of over forty minutes, uncharacteristically long for "Silent Cal." Press reports described the speech without passion, much as Coolidge had delivered it. Yet one feature of the address was remarkable. For the first time, the ceremony, including the address, was broadcast on the radio to an estimated twenty million people. The crowd at the Capitol applauded with good spirit; Coolidge left the stand before the applause had concluded.

History books have referred derisively to "Coolidge prosperity." Many segments of society did well during his administration but real wages dropped and a sizable number of Americans bought into the stock market paying as little as 10% of the cost in cash. Credit captured America's fancy in the 1920s. Personally, though, Coolidge's values did not include making money by gambling with someone else's money. Gain was to be made by one's own hard work.

How ironic, then, that the Puritan Yankee's name should become associated with an economy about to collapse. How fortunate for him that he chose not to run again in 1928, withdrawing himself from the race in August 1927. The untidinesses known as the "Crash of '29 " and "The Great Depression" were someone else's to handle. The nation's values with regard to gain strayed far from the Puritan virtues of hard work. Was Coolidge's official statement in 1923 about God directing destiny accurate after all?

Herbert Hoover

Following Calvin Coolidge to office was a man with a marvelous resume and terrible luck. Though widely and highly regarded for his administrative success organizing humanitarian efforts during World War I, Herbert Hoover's name would become linked to newspaper blankets and shanty town-Hoovervilles by unemployed and homeless Americans. Winning more votes for President than any man previously, Hoover could little know that a mere 239 days after pledging to "preserve, protect and defend the Constitution of the United States," the Great Crash of 1929 would occur, precipitating this country's severest economic depression.

Those looking for omens could find them in the events of March 4, 1929. Heavy rain fell periodically throughout the day. Inclement weather had beset past inaugurations, but in this day's events there was a special nemesis, wind. A cover built so that the President and his party could remain dry during the ceremony proved useless as the wind drove the rain horizontally, soaking even those under the cover.

Additionally, the wives of the two Presidents, Coolidge and Hoover, got lost in the Capitol as they proceeded from the Senate Chamber where Vice President Curtis had been sworn in. That delayed Hoover's inauguration. They had to ask directions to get out, which they eventually did.

Finally, the President-elect had chosen to have the family Bible open to Matthew 5, the Sermon on the Mount. In those memorable passages, Jesus praises the humble, the peacemakers and the merciful and articulates the vision adopted by the Puritans for America, that of a "city on a hill." But the confusion over the first ladies led to the Bible being opened in haste, at random, to the book of Proverbs. Chief Justice Taft recited the words of the oath of office and Herbert Hoover became the 31st President by saying "I do" with his fingers resting on Proverbs 29:18. "Where there is no vision, the people perish: but he that keepeth the law, happy is he."

Though a Quaker born in the Midwest and educated at Stanford, Hoover demonstrated lifelong virtues wholly consistent with his Puritan New England predecessor. An orphan, Hoover worked diligently to win admission to Stanford and graduated in its first class as a mining engineer. He earned great respect and world-wide reputation, as well as financial success before he was thirty. What Hoover did especially well was to organize. When World War I created emergency relief needs in Europe, Hoover directed the American Relief Committee in London and was Commissioner for Belgium Relief. From 1917 to 1919, he also served as U.S. Food Administrator. By 1920 his reputation as a talented manager was unique in the world. The Democratic Party responded by asking him to be part of their national ticket in 1920. Hoover declined.

Only then did Hoover declare his affiliation with the Republican Party. When President Harding assembled in his Cabinet "the best Republican minds," Hoover became Secretary of Commerce. He reorganized and expanded that department during the decade when business interests reigned supreme, serving both President Harding and President Coolidge. Because he had carefully constructed a political organization in support of his candidacy, Hoover capitalized quickly on President Coolidge's decision not to run in 1928, and he won the Republican nomination on the first ballot. In the Electoral College, Hoover won 40 states to New York Governor Al Smith's eight.

Then came the Great Crash. President Hoover carried a conservative and traditional economic philosophy. According to that orthodoxy, economic downturns were cyclical; U.S. history had proved them so. Time combined with rugged individuals who worked hard to hold themselves and their families together were the major factors in recovery. Government had a role to play primarily in stimulating business and protecting American goods from foreign competition through high tariffs. However, Hoover rejected the idea that government ought to provide jobs or direct relief to individuals, and he embraced the belief that problems are best solved at the state and local level. President Hoover adhered to these laws of economics which he saw as immutable. He had lived through the Depression of the 1890s, the worst that the nation had seen to that point and, indeed, had realized much success as a mining engineer during that period. The nation survived that depression following the old laws; it had even successfully won a world war. President Hoover's experiences and beliefs rendered him incapable of accepting any new vision of how the government ought to respond to the economic crisis at hand.

President Hoover's was the first inauguration ever to be recorded in a film with sound. Listeners heard a pedantic call for the status quo. As President, Hoover enjoyed little of the status quo. Three and a half years after the Great Crash, the voters swept Hoover from office by a 3 to 1 margin (9 to 1 in the Electoral College). A new President, one not tied to belief in immutable laws but a grand experimenter who spoke of a new vision, came to power. Right or not, the people chose an expression of vision over one who "kept the law."

Franklin D. Roosevelt

On March 4, 1933, Franklin D. Roosevelt took the oath of office to become the thirty-second President, the last to be inaugurated so long after the election. By virtue of the Twentieth Amendment, the President's term in the future would begin at noon on January 20, the date on which Roosevelt repeated the oath in 1937, 1941 and 1945. Each time, the Dutch Bible brought to America three hundred years before by his ancestors was opened to 1 Corinthians, 13.

"And now abideth faith, hope, charity, these three; but the greatest of these is charity," reads the final verse of the chapter. This oft-quoted scripture directs its readers to think about how people interact with one another. Whether one reads the King James or more modern translations which substitute the word "love" for "charity," the lesson remains constant. We are at our best when our focus is on others, not ourselves.

When Roosevelt came to office in 1933, the nation needed doses of all three: faith, hope and charity. In his first Inaugural Address, President Roosevelt counseled the nation that "the only thing we have to fear is fear itself -- nameless, unreasoning, unjustified terror which paralyzes needed efforts to convert retreat into advance." Following his inauguration with swift proposals and Congressional approvals, Roosevelt elicited faith in his administration and rekindled hope to replace fear in the people

The crisis abated only very slowly, but steadily. In the election of 1934, President Roosevelt's Democratic Party majority in Congress increased and in 1936, he won a victory over Alf Landon rivaled in its magnitude only by the unanimous vote won by President Washington and the landslide by James Monroe in 1820. Of course, Roosevelt won twice more as well.

President Roosevelt assumed office, not as an ideologue with any sweeping vision of society but as a pragmatist, willing to try anything that might work. A major component of his early program was the National Recovery Administration encouraging collaboration among businesses which, in other times, might be criticized as trusts or monopolies. The Agricultural Adjustment Act paid farmers not to grow certain products, a significant departure of philosophy for the relationship of the farmer and the government. Neither idea was Roosevelt's alone; he depended heavily on the thoughts and proposals of others. Similarly, FDR, a believer in balanced budgets, came to accept the economic philosophy of John Maynard Keynes which accepted deficit spending as a means to stimulate a depressed economy. And his early programs for relief blended government jobs with direct welfare payments to people, the first such program in our nation's history.

"For now we see through a glass darkly, then face to face..." The twelfth verse of 1 Corinthians 13 proclaims a great optimism; one day we shall know what we now do not know. Such was Roosevelt's nature. Well might he have been optimistic in his early life. Born into wealth and social prominence, he was educated at prestigious schools (Groton, then Harvard), was cousin to a President and was successful in his first government post as Assistant Secretary of the Navy in the Wilson Administration throughout World War One. His service and pedigree earned him the Vice Presidential spot on the Democratic ticket in 1920. Though he lost, Roosevelt looked at a bright political future.

Then came polio. For the next several years, Roosevelt's struggles were personal, not political. In the 1920's, crippled legs crippled futures. Roosevelt saw differently, and in 1928, he returned to politics to win the Governorship of New York. Immediately, he became a leading candidate for his party's nomination in 1932 as his predecessor, Al Smith, had been in 1928. Given the circumstances of the Depression, winning the Democratic nomination was tantamount to winning the general election in November.

President Roosevelt's willingness to accept federal government programs in direct support of the people and to regulate various sectors of the economy forever altered the scope and power of the national government. Likewise, his deft use of radio, capitalizing on a strong, reassuring voice, shifted the balance between the branches of government. What Presidents said and how they said it were regarded differently after his administration. The President became Chief Problem-Solver, the true energy in national government.

This vision of energy and strength was reinforced by an incident at the second inauguration. The *New York Times* reported: "Then his responded [to the oath]. There was no trace of the famous campaign smile. His strong jaw came out; his strong, vibrant voice resounded over the rain-drenched throng and was carried resonantly to the far island territories and to ships at sea by the mechanistic miracle of radio."

"Not content was he to say 'I do.' Instead, he repeated the oath verbatim, emphasizing by his manner and by his voice the words 'Constitution,' 'preserve, protect and defend,' and bearing down hard on the word 'domestic,' as contrasted with foreign enemies."

"It was a moment to be remembered. At the risk of being trite, one might say that it was not what was said but the way in which it was said. The emphasis was not lost upon the crowd. Under the umbrellas men and women turned to one another. They understood." [36]

Roosevelt spoke, in that second Inaugural Address, of the need to restore the nation and its people to prosperity. Of course, he delivered the speech standing up, on braced legs which could not alone hold him up. His hands delivered his tremendous upper body strength to the task of steadying himself on the podium. For his own political benefit and as a symbol of confidence for the nation, President Roosevelt was not photographed as crippled. He had overcome infirmity. So would the nation.

By 1940, new enemies, ones foreign, had arisen. Our allies were at war. In his third Inaugural Address, President Roosevelt preached preparedness, cautiously, by warning against the dangers of isolationism. Before repeating the oath a third time on January 20, 1941, the President attended services at St. John's Episcopal Church where he recited scripture, Psalms 20: 7-8. "Some trust in chariots, and some in horses; but we will remember the name of the Lord, our God. They are brought down and fallen; but we are risen, and stand upright."

Roosevelt's election to a third term broke American political precedent. An 85% tally in the Electoral College suggested that the voters cared little about that precedent. Within a year, the United States was itself a combatant in the second World War, and President Roosevelt was again preaching faith and hope. At war in 1944, the nation elected Roosevelt to a fourth term by a slightly smaller landslide (81% in the Electoral College) in an election where the main drama was over the President's choice of a running mate. For that job, Roosevelt selected the Senator from Missouri, Harry Truman. Less than three months after the inauguration of January 20, 1945, President Roosevelt died.

People responded emotionally to Franklin Roosevelt. Those who loved him, and the election returns suggested that many did, valued his strength and confidence and saw his "New Deal" as successful. Those who disliked him called him "that man in the White House." In political discourse, the New Deal sparks similar impassioned debate; did it help the nation to recover, or did it create a massively oppressive, and ultimately ineffective, governmental bureaucracy? Whatever the assessment, there is little doubt that the intent of President Roosevelt's domestic policies was born of the spirit of charity, the desire for the well-being of all citizens. Nor is there doubt that faith and hope, in two periods of crisis, one domestic, the other foreign, found voice in the strong and resonant tones of Franklin Roosevelt.

Harry Truman

Early in the afternoon of April 13, 1945, Harry Truman met reporters in a hallway at the Capitol. "Boys," he said, "if you ever pray, pray for me now. I don't know whether you fellows ever had a load of hay fall on you, but when they told me yesterday what had happened, I felt like the moon, the stars, and all the planets had fallen on me." No astronomical fallout had occurred on April 12, but a heavy load did weigh down Truman's shoulders. He became President, less than three months after becoming Vice President, succeeding a larger-than-life figure who had steered the country through a severe economic depression and a soon-to-be-completed world war.

Truman had been called to the White House at 5:00 p.m. on April 12, not knowing what was wanted. Two hours later, he was President. In the Cabinet Room the Chief Justice had assembled along with several Congressional leaders, most members of the Cabinet and the Vice President's wife and daughter. As David McCullough described the scene, a call went out for a Bible. The only one to be found "was an inexpensive Gideon edition with garish red edging to the pages." Truman later said that "he could have brought Grandpa Truman's Bible from his office bookcase had he only known." [37]

The closed Bible in his hand, Truman swore the oath as administered by Chief Justice Harlan Stone. "The sudden, fervent way he kissed the Bible at the end of the ceremony impressed everyone present. It had all taken not more than a minute." [38]

Harry Truman was the seventh man to succeed to the office upon the death of his predecessor. None before had faced such trying times. Within the first four months, he would decide to use the atomic bomb, accept the surrender of Germany and Japan, fulfill FDR's dream of U.S. leadership in the forming of the United Nations, and so offend Joseph Stalin that personal animosity joined philosophical disagreement as a key ingredient in the beginning of the Cold War.

Many in 1945 regarded Harry Truman as just another machine politician whose cronies would soon invade Washington, resulting in a repeat of the Harding scandals. Others knew better. Truman possessed a commendable record as a combat officer in World War I, and had earned a reputation as an honest and independent County Court Judge in spite of starting his political career as a favorite of the local Democratic boss, Harry Pendergast. His Senate Select Committee on defense spending won respect for its careful and judicious investigation. Those who know him valued his honesty, decisiveness and strong passion for history. Though he came to office without the benefit of Roosevelt ever having discussed foreign affairs with him, two of his earliest decisions - to proceed with the United Nations conference and to personally invite the Soviet Foreign Minister -- were common sense choices absolutely correct in the circumstances. President Truman, his friends knew, would have no trouble making the tough decisions.

Thomas Dewey learned about Truman's tenacity in the election of 1948. Bitter political battles and the start of the Cold War marked President Truman's first term. So dismal were Democratic prospects in the spring of 1948 that Truman, himself, along with the rest of the party leadership didn't much covet the Presidential nomination. Truman ran because no one else would. The patrician Governor Dewey of New York led the Republicans during their fall march to seemingly certain victory.

In its November 3, 1948 edition the *Chicago Tribune* proclaimed victory for Dewey. Truman went to bed on election night believing he had lost. The people voted otherwise, however. Truman possessed the common touch, the ability to reach beyond power and position to connect with common folk. All knew Truman's roots were humble. People understood his plain speaking. "Give 'em hell, Harry," shouted ever-growing numbers of supporters at train stops during the campaign. In spite of a party splintered by the candidacies of segregationist

Governor Thurmond and liberal Henry Wallace, Truman won 38 states and 57% of the electoral vote.

On January 20, 1949, President Truman celebrated his beginning of a second term. There were more victory parties than in any previous inaugural week. The President attended many of the events and, characteristically, even found time for a breakfast with members of his World War I army unit. Truman's was the first inauguration to be televised live. What viewers saw was the President on a clear, cold day repeating the oath of office using not one, but two Bibles. The first was open to Matthew 5, the Sermon on the Mount. For the second, Truman chose Exodus 20, the Ten Commandments.

The commandments are simple and direct, stipulating the duty of God's children. The Sermon on the Mount praises humility and mercy and translates aspects of the Ten Commandments into requirements of righteous thought. Truman seemed to embody simplicity, duty and humility. Matthew described Christ as praising his listeners as the "salt of the earth." Truman's advocates have described him as such.

President Truman's second term saw many more tense moments in world affairs; the Berlin blockade, the fall of China, the Korean War. In domestic matters, as well, President Truman met with mixed success. Yet the United States under Truman did assume leadership of the free world and enjoyed a surprisingly robust economy with broad sections of society sharing in the prosperity. In the Truman years, the nation became that city on a hill described by Jesus, and desired by the Puritan Governor Winthrop three hundred years before.

Dwight D. Eisenhower

Dwight D. Eisenhower took the oath of office on Tuesday, January 20, 1953 from Chief Justice Fred Vinson with his hand over two Bibles. One belonged to history, the one used by George Washington, now opened to Psalms 127:1. The second was from Ike's cadet days at West Point. It was opened to 2 Chronicles 7:14. Eisenhower made both choices. "Except the Lord build the house, they labour in vain that build it; except the Lord keep the city, the watchman waketh but in vain." So read the Psalm selection of the latest military hero to be elected President.

2 Chronicles offers a promise. "If my people, which are called by my name, shall humble themselves, and pray, and seek my face, and turn from their wicked ways; then will I hear from heaven and will forgive their sin, and will heal their land." Though Eisenhower's beginnings were, indeed, humble, by 1953 he had commanded the largest naval invasion in history, earning the credit for winning World War Two. He had also led an outstanding research university and served as the founding general of one of the most ambitious alliances ever, NATO.

Yet he was perceived to be humble even still, the genial grandfather to the country, easy of temper, possessed of a winning smile and a penchant for golf. When he began his Inaugural Address with a prayer of his own composition, the first ever to do so, the thirty-fourth President fulfilled another of the conditions set in 2 Chronicles. The

President then went on to make plain his hopes for an administration marked by peace, at home and abroad.

The idea for the prayer came to him as he returned to his hotel from an Inauguration Day worship service at National Presbyterian Church. As Eisenhower wrote in his memoir, he did not want his "Inaugural Address to be a sermon..." But, he continued, he carried a "deep faith in the beneficence of the Almighty" from his childhood days in Kansas. And, he sought "a way to point out that we [the U.S.] were getting too secular." His wife, Mamie, his "son and daughter-in-law, and one or two close friends" were his trial audience before he delivered his prayer to the nation. {39]

Eisenhower took office with the United States at war with the Chinese and North Koreans and the domestic front divided by the poison of McCarthyism. In his first Inaugural Address, he described the world as divided into the masses of good and the masses of evil. He asked rhetorically how far mankind had come from the darkness toward the light and listed the assets which had been accumulated by the forces of light. What America needed to do, he said, was to proclaim its faith in the "deathless dignity of man."

To frame the issues facing the world and the U.S. in 1953 in terms of combat would be natural for this lifelong soldier. Immensely popular following the victory in World War Two, Eisenhower could have had the nomination of either political party. No one actually knew his party affiliation until he turned down the overtures of the Democratic Party in 1952 and allowed his name to be on the ballot for the Republican primary in New Hampshire. Winning the Republican nomination proved a greater challenge than defeating the Democratic candidate, Adlai Stevenson, in November. Eisenhower won 55% of the popular vote and 83% of the Electoral College vote.

As if to underscore the point that Eisenhower's personal popularity elected him President, nowhere did the rest of the Republican Party do as well. By 1954, the GOP had lost the slim majorities they had enjoyed in both houses of Congress.

Eisenhower called his first memoir *Mandate for Change*. Certainly, his electoral majority suggested that the citizenry wanted something different. Ike was the first Republican to occupy the White House in twenty years. The new President's clearest message on January 20, 1953 concerned foreign affairs. Unequivocally, he stated, the United

States would exercise a leadership role in world affairs, leading the forces of light, the masses of good. That was a different message from a Republican President than had been heard since Theodore Roosevelt. Who better to lead the leading nation of the free world than the winning general in the last war?

There was little to suggest in Eisenhower's early life that he would come to occupy such a lofty position in the minds of his countrymen and women. He struggled to gain admission to the U.S. Military Academy, graduated in the middle of the class and came to World War One too late to gain any combat experience of note. His most impressive job in the Army before World War Two was as General Douglas MacArthur's aide in Washington and then the Philippines. But, once the war began, he attracted the eye of General George Marshall for his work in planning a set of war games in Louisiana, and that attention got him a command in North Africa. Success there led to the Normandy invasion assignment and the great acclaim which followed.

By his second Inauguration Day, 1957, the tense peace of the Cold War characterized world affairs and Americans at home were relatively prosperous. At this swearing-in, accomplished privately in the White House on Sunday, January 20, 1957, and publicly in ceremonies the next day, President Eisenhower used another passage from Psalms in a Bible given to him by his Mother, Psalms 33:12. "Blessed is the nation whose God is the Lord; and the people whom he hath chosen for his own inheritance."

From the warning about vain labour in 1953 to the blessed nation and people in 1957, the country did, indeed change under Eisenhower's watch, at least in the President's eyes. *Waging Peace* became the title for a second volume of memoirs, a clever use of a verb normally associated with war.

Momentous change was brewing domestically following the 1954 Supreme Court decision in *Brown v. Board of Education*, fueling the great civil rights accomplishments of the 1960s. But integration attempts sparked confrontation during the Eisenhower years without producing needed legislation. Similarly, the Russian launching of Sputnik into space in 1957 spawned a further set of unsettling anxieties which disturbed the tranquillity of Eisenhower's second term. In the collective mind of the country, America was falling behind in the space race, and race relations were fractious. The peace we enjoyed was an uneasy one at best.

President Eisenhower's prayer in 1953 had been "for all the people regardless of station, race or calling." When Ike left office in 1961, social justice for all was only a dream. But the people still loved Eisenhower. He'd kept the peace. President Eisenhower retired to his farm in Gettysburg, Pennsylvania content that, to the best of his ability, by the grace and with the aid of the Lord, he had done his duty.

John F. Kennedy

The new President concluded, "With a good conscience our only sure reward, with history the final judge of our deeds, let us go forth to lead the land we love, asking His blessing and His help, but knowing that here on earth, God's work must truly be our own." Far more memorable lines from this most famous Inaugural Address proclaimed that the "torch of leadership" had been "passed to a new generation" and asked citizens to consider not what their country could do for them but what they could do for their country.

Few inaugurations have marked such a dramatic shift in age between the old and the new Presidents. John F. Kennedy was sworn in at age 43, succeeding a man who was 71. The first President to be born in the 20th century, Kennedy brought to office an excitement and energy intended to infuse the nation with renewed enthusiasm for America's leadership role in the world. For the first time in the twentieth century, a President had children under the age of ten; they added to the charm of a White House deliberate in its cultivation of charm as a political asset. Yet domestic divisions and foreign threats reminded the men and women of Kennedy's New Frontier of the realities of the world, tempering the optimism of January 20, 1961 within but a few short months.

John Kennedy came to be President by virtue of his own accomplishment and some effective and clever political groundwork. Born to a rich family and educated at prestigious schools, Kennedy

served in the Navy in World War Two. In an episode made famous in a
popular song of the early 1960s, Kennedy became a hero when his boat,
PT-109, was sunk by the Japanese and he helped to save some of his
fellow sailors. He returned to Boston to run for the House of
Representatives. He moved on to the Senate in 1952 and was an
unsuccessful, but noticed, candidate for the vice-presidential nomination
at the 1956 Democratic Convention. By 1960, Kennedy and his people
had mapped out a strategy for winning key primaries which would
produce the nomination for him. Then, an equally well-calculated
strategy earned him a narrow victory over Republican Richard Nixon.

Several special Kennedy touches highlighted his inauguration.
Mindful that his Catholicism had been potentially damaging to him in
the campaign and fostered lingering suspicions in the imagination of
those distrustful of the Pope, President Kennedy included three prayers
before he spoke, one by a Catholic, one by a Greek Orthodox, the third
by a Disciples of Christ preacher. Ever the intellectual, the President
asked poet Robert Frost to read a poem at the ceremony which, because
of too-brilliant light, he was unable to do. Instead, Frost recited "The
Gift Outright." As the President-elect repeated the oath administered by
Chief Justice Earl Warren, he inadvertently removed his hand from the
family's Douay version of the Bible, leaving it at his side and prompting
inquiries about whether the swearing-in was legal because he did so. Then
came the stirring speech, one of the two or three most-often quoted
Inaugural Addresses ever given.

Something else unique occurred. The first clergyman to pray was
Richard Cardinal Cushing of Boston. As he prayed, smoke emanated
from beneath the inaugural stand. The Chief of the Secret Service detail
nearly cleared the stand three times before the smoke stopped. Cardinal
Cushing noticed the smoke, too. Fearing that the smoke came from a
smoldering bomb, the Cardinal drew out his phrases and sentences,
resolved to be a human shield for the President in case the explosive
detonated. Those who heard the Cardinal only thought him tedious.
None knew his motives. As it turned out, a faulty electrical connection
caused the smoke. [40]

The first quotation of scripture by the President came as he listed
the ways in which both sides, meaning the United States and the Soviet
Union, might "begin anew the quest for peace." "Let both sides unite to
heed in all corners of the earth the command of Isaiah--to 'undo the

heavy burden...and to let the oppressed go free.'" President Kennedy's references to Isaiah 58:6 reflected the nation's fixation on the authoritarian communist regimes in Eastern Europe but especially the Soviet Union.

The President had campaigned using the claim of a missile gap, ostensibly leaving the U.S. vulnerable to Soviet attack. At the close of the previous administration, an American reconnaissance pilot had been shot down and imprisoned in the USSR, and the nearby island nation of Cuba had come under the rule of a Communist dictator. The Soviets had reached space before the U.S. with its Sputnik satellite, had made noisy threats against us in the United Nations, and had frightened many Americans into building bomb shelters in their backyards. For the President now to call for the freeing of the oppressed was consistent with the Cold War view the U.S. carried about the world.

President Kennedy's brief administration featured several episodes where the "quest for peace" by the two superpowers was a central concern: the Bay of Pigs invasion, the Berlin Wall, the Cuban Missile Crisis, the communist insurgency in Laos and Vietnam, the nuclear test ban treaty. On the domestic front, his Isaiah reference carried significance as well, in the civil rights movement which demanded that "the oppressed go free." Each of those "heavy burdens" taxed the bright young men and women of the New Frontier in their time at the helm, producing moments of tension, triumph, defeat and hope.

In calling on his countrymen to bear the various burdens he identified, President Kennedy asked that the people be "rejoicing in hope, patient in tribulation." This verse from Romans 12:12 concludes with "continuing instant in prayer." The President could not have guessed that the nation would find great tribulation in the circumstances of his own death.

President Kennedy was shot and killed in Dallas, Texas on November 22, 1963. He was the fourth Chief Executive to be assassinated, but the first in an age when news of the killing would be communicated instantly nation- and world-wide. The shock was instant and deep. President Kennedy's impact globally was such that his death was grieved around the world.

Eighty-two years earlier, upon the death of President Garfield, Americans were told that "there are mysteries we cannot penetrate. Divine purpose is known to God alone." All America knew was that the hopeful rejoicing of January 1961 had become the tribulation of November 1963. The leader of the "new generation" to whom the torch had been passed had given all for his country that he could; his life.

Lyndon Johnson

A photograph powerful to those who lived through the transition from President Kennedy to President Johnson underscores the importance placed on the presence of the Bible for our swearings-in. Johnson, his wife, Lady Bird, and the President's widow, Jacqueline, stand before District Judge Sarah Hughes. The Vice President's right hand is raised and the left rests on a black book. It is a closed Catholic prayer book, the closest to a Bible available on Air Force One November 22, 1963. The new President would not proceed without a Bible or some reasonable substitute.

Following the taking of the oath, President Johnson said nothing for the public record until the plane landed at Andrews Air Force Base and the coffin had been sent on its way to Bethesda Naval Hospital. "This is a sad time for all people," the President said at Andrews. "We have suffered a loss that cannot be weighed. For me, it is a deep personal tragedy. I know the world shares the sorrow that Mrs. Kennedy and her family bear. I will do my best. That is all I can do. I ask for your help---and God's." President Johnson's first Inaugural Address said all that could be said to a nation stunned by the death of its young President.

Tragedy of a different sort awaited President Johnson. Elected by the highest percentage of the popular vote ever, 61%, and triumphant early in Congress with many of his Great Society programs, President Johnson left office haunted by a protracted and unpopular war. The man who hoped to be remembered as the architect of a new social order characterized by equality and an end to poverty retired to his ranch in Texas more known for his consistent support of South Vietnam in its struggle to avoid defeat by guerilla insurgents and North Vietnam.

President Johnson came to the White House a seasoned and skillful political leader. First elected to Congress in 1936, Johnson won a Senate seat in 1948 and rose to become the Majority Leader during the Eisenhower Administration. Johnson, Speaker of the House Sam Rayburn and President Eisenhower forged a working relationship despite party differences which produced such remarkable legislation as the first Civil Rights Act (1957) since the 1870s, weak though it seemed when compared to later ones.

A candidate for the White House himself during the primaries of 1960, Johnson accepted Kennedy's offer to create a political alliance between the Northeast and the South and won the Vice Presidency. Often subordinating his own personal feelings, and sometimes scorned as inelegant and coarse compared to the Kennedy clan, Johnson served President Kennedy loyally and helped the President through several difficult situations with Congress.

President Johnson's 1964 opponent, Senator Barry Goldwater of Arizona, came from the conservative wing of the Republican Party and stood little chance against the more centrist Johnson who carried the mantle of the fallen leader. The inauguration of 1965 offered the President the opportunity to be acclaimed in his own right, to come out from under the shadow of John Kennedy. Johnson's natural country-boy quality contrasted sharply with the Boston-Harvard air of the Kennedy Administration, and when he chose to be sworn in wearing a business suit rather than a top hat and tails, he made the distinction vividly clear.

Likewise, the gusto with which he threw himself into dancing and partying at the Inaugural Balls separated Johnson from his more sedate predecessor, and reinforced his "good ole boy" image.

Inviting friends and neighbors with impunity, President Johnson set out to make the days around January 20, 1965 a celebration without parallel. Receptions, galas, dinners, a concert followed by a party and dance; all this fun led up to Inauguration Day. The morning of the ceremony, the President, a member of the Disciples of Christ denomination, and his entourage participated in a worship service at

National City Christian Church. The service featured Protestant, Catholic and Jewish clergy in an unprecedented interfaith program. Under clear and sunny skies, the inauguration itself included prayers from the Archbishop of San Antonio, a Houston Rabbi and a Protestant minister from Washington D.C.

With his hand on the Bible presented to the President and Lady Bird by his mother, held by his wife (the first to do so), Lyndon Johnson took the oath of office for a second time. Chief Justice Warren administered the oath. The thirty-sixth President turned to address the nation which had elected him so decisively.

"My fellow countrymen," he began. "On this occasion, the oath I have taken before you and before God, is not mine alone but ours together." Thus he sought unity in the nation. The President continued by centering his speech around the concept of covenant, an idea key to America since the Pilgrims signed the Mayflower Compact. The President described the Compact as "conceived in justice, written in liberty, bound in union...meant one day to inspire the hopes of all mankind, and it binds us still." "Under this covenant of justice, liberty and union, we have become a nation prosperous, great and mighty...But we have no promise from God that our greatness will endure." Then he called for his Great Society, a series of social programs aimed at improving the economic and political lot of the underclass in America.

The President once remarked that if he hadn't been a politician, he'd have been a preacher, and his address had much of the structure and substance of a sermon. In conclusion, he recalled his promise in the first address---"I will lead and I will do the best I can." Then he repeated the request of Solomon in 2 Chronicles 1:10. "Give me now wisdom and knowledge that I may go out and come in before this people: for who can judge this, thy people, that is so great?"

To Solomon, the Lord God responded, "Wisdom and knowledge is granted unto thee; and I will give thee riches, and wealth, and honour, such as none of the kings that have been before thee." (2 Chronicles 1:12) President Johnson was less fortunate. While several of the individual programs proposed by the President passed, the Great Society he envisioned as the triumph of our American covenant fell victim to war in Vietnam. And the President himself suffered the consequences of pursuing that war which increasing numbers of Americans refused to support.

Richard M. Nixon

Isaiah 2:4 reads: "And he shall judge among the nations, and shall rebuke many people; and they shall beat their swords into plowshares, and their spears into pruning hooks: nation shall not lift up sword against nation, neither shall they learn war anymore." If one were to speculate on meaningful scripture to Quakers, surely, this would be one. Quaker Richard Nixon repeated his oath of office to become our 37th President with his hand on two Bibles opened to Isaiah 2:4. His wife, Pat, held the two Bibles for his first inauguration as President on January 20, 1969 as she had in 1953 and 1957 when he took the oath as Vice President. She repeated the act in 1973.

President Nixon's choice of Isaiah carried other significance as well. It was the favorite of his mother, Hannah, who carried great influence in Nixon's life well beyond her death. Some historians, in fact, have asserted that President Nixon's personal conflicts resulted from the clash of his father's harsh, combative personality with his mother's gentle, peaceful Quakerism. To honor her at the moment of his greatest personal achievement by selecting her favorite verse would have been understandable.

Additionally, the President came into office when the war in Vietnam was the dominant political issue. Perhaps there was a further personal significance, too. President Nixon could view his various political struggles in dramatic, even warlike imagery. One of his books about his career he entitled *Six Great Crises*. Could not this rather tragic figure in U.S. history have yearned for peace in one part of his being while brandishing his political sword with another?

Richard Nixon's political biography became more well known to Americans than most Presidents' because his demise in office was a drawn-out affair televised to the nation. Nixon was a veteran of World War Two service in the Navy when he ran for Congress in 1946 and unseated an incumbent. In that campaign, Nixon succeeded in creating doubt about the incumbent's loyalty to America, a pattern of campaigning he used successfully again when he won his U.S. Senate seat in 1950. The young politician capitalized on generalized fears in the nation of the growth of communism internationally, and his personal following was such that he was selected as a regional balance on the Eisenhower ticket in 1952, though he was the junior Senator from California.

Thus, he came to the Presidency with an impressive political resume, including his eight years as Vice President. Nixon knew defeat, too, having lost to John Kennedy in a close election in 1960 and to Pat Brown for the California Governorship in 1962. After the 1962 loss, Nixon practiced law in New York and began several years of hard work in behalf of his party's candidates in 1964 and 1966. Hard work characterized Nixon in all of his endeavors. His industriousness in behalf of Republicans produced valuable political IOUs, which he used to advantage in the race for the nomination in 1968.

In the quest for the 1968 nomination, Nixon's allies spoke of a "new Nixon," one less shrill and combative, more statesmanlike. During the campaign, Nixon claimed to have a plan to end U.S. involvement in Vietnam in a "peace with honor." His strategy for election included a deliberate appeal for Southern votes, too, unusual for a Republican. The South had voted solidly Democratic since the Civil War. The strategy worked, establishing a shift in political party preference which has continued well past his Presidency. And his Inauguration Address in 1969 developed themes of peace and reconciliation aimed both domestically and internationally.

How ironic, then, the circumstances of his fall. While achieving an American disengagement in Vietnam, opening dialogue with the People's Republic of China and establishing a *détente* in relations with the Soviet Union, Nixon's supporters engaged in a series of illegal activities aimed at the President's political enemies. When the

President learned of a failed break-in at the Watergate Office Complex, he muffed his chance to avoid the subsequent unraveling of his Presidency by seeking to avoid embarrassment. How history might have been different if President Nixon had reported to the nation the errors of his political operatives in 1972 rather than opting to cover them up!

How tragic the result. In addition to the foreign policy successes, President Nixon registered significant accomplishments on the home front as well. His early choices for the Supreme Court, Warren Burger and Harry Blackmun, proved to be effective and well-respected justices. Revenue-sharing, using the Federal Government to collect money then send it to the state for use as they saw fit was a bold new policy initiative, and he was the first President to use wage-price freezes in peacetime as a way to combat inflation. (Official peace, that is; Vietnam was still a police action.) The space program prospered, new taxation features helped poor people and important environmental legislation was enacted. Acutely aware of history, Nixon gained successes as President which could have produced high praise from future observers had they not the burden of viewing his administration through the lens of the Watergate scandal.

President Nixon's second inaugural followed by days the cease-fire in Vietnam. But the heat of the Watergate investigation flamed even then. Within three months, the Senate Select Committee on Watergate began its hearings; within six months, the existence of recordings of Oval Office conversations became known. By December, 1973, the President was reduced to claiming "I am not a crook" to a televised audience. In July, 1974, the Supreme Court ruled 9-0 that he had to turn over the tapes of the White House conversations to the Special Prosecutor investigating Watergate and shortly thereafter, the House Judiciary Committee voted Articles of Impeachment. On August 9, 1974, Richard Nixon became the first to resign the Presidency of the United States.

In his first Inaugural Address, President Nixon quoted the Old Testament prophet, Malachi. "But unto you that fear my name shall the Sun of righteousness arise with healing in his wings; and ye shall go forth, and grow up as calves of the stall." (Malachi 4:2) The "new Nixon" of reconciliation and healing fell, conquered, perhaps, by President Nixon's own inability to stop warring politically. The nation shared in Nixon's tragedy, enduring a devastating ordeal in which we learned again not to trust what our leaders told us, a legacy started by the Vietnam conflict. Gerald Ford assumed office by proclaiming "the long national nightmare [to be] over." How sad that the "Sun of righteousness" faded into a bad dream, for President Nixon and for his countrymen.

Gerald R. Ford

"Trust in the Lord with all thine heart; and lean not unto thine own understanding. In all ways acknowledge him, and he shall direct thy paths." (Proverbs 3:5-6) In a 1992 interview with Walter Cronkite, Gerald R. Ford, 38th President, described these verses as a passage he had "loved and turned to" many times in his life. No surprise to those who knew him well, then, that these words rested beneath his hand when he took the oath of office on August 9, 1974. His wife, Betty, held the Bible while Chief Justice Warren Burger administered the oath. Eight times before, Vice Presidents had taken up the Presidency in the middle of a term, but always at the death of the incumbent. And those eight had won election as Vice President.

Gerald Ford recognized his special status in the very first line of his first speech as President. "I am acutely aware that you have not elected me as your President by your ballots...I have not sought this enormous responsibility, but I will not shirk it." He found himself in the East Room that noon by virtue of the 25th Amendment to the Constitution. The Vice President elected in 1972, Spiro T. Agnew, had resigned, and President Nixon, acting under the amendment added only ten years before, had nominated the leader of the Republican minority in the House of Representatives. Nixon believed Ford to be a safe bet to be confirmed by his legislative colleagues to replace Agnew. Ford took office December 6, 1973, then succeeded President Nixon only nine months later.

For twenty-four years, Ford had represented Michigan's Fifth Congressional District in the House. A talented football player for the University of Michigan in the 1930s, a Yale Law School graduate in 1941, and a naval officer in the Pacific during World War Two, Ford beat an entrenched incumbent in the Republican primary in 1948 then cruised to victory in November. His victory was overshadowed by the surprising win by President Harry Truman over Thomas E. Dewey. Ford settled in to build a reputation as something between a moderate and a conservative, well-schooled in defense issues, a loyal Eisenhower Republican. Most of his legislative career was spent as a member of the minority party. In 1965, he became the leader of the Republicans in the House, defeating the incumbent, Charles Halleck. The only higher office Ford wanted was the Speaker's job.

Ford loved the House. Twice in speeches to the Gridiron Club, in 1969 and again in 1974, (when he *was* the Vice President), he said "I'm not at all interested in the Vice Presidency. I love the House of Representatives, despite the long, irregular hours." [41] Colleagues knew him to be a party loyalist yet one who understood that the dynamic of American politics is compromise. Under Ford, the House Republicans were never obstructionist but always a tough loyal opposition.

Words like *hardworking, honest, decent* and *trustworthy* abound in descriptions of Gerald Ford. Some credited his Midwestern stock, born and raised as he was among stern Dutch Calvinists in Grand Rapids, Michigan. Ford's family was Episcopalian, less restrictive in their beliefs than the Calvinists, and one of the centers of activity for the family was Grace Episcopal Church. The future President's early training spawned a daily habit of prayer in high school. When faced with tough decisions, like the one to pardon President Nixon, President Ford often spoke of having prayed about the situation before deciding. Indeed, Ford seemed to "lean not unto [his] own understanding."

In his short Inaugural Address, President Ford reassured the nation that "Our Constitution works." A period of collective relief came over the country, and President Ford enjoyed the credit he received for that relief. With the pardon on September 8, 1974, Ford's own tribulations began; accusations of a deal with Nixon at the time of the resignation and charges that he placed Nixon above the law. Undoubtedly, President Ford had misjudged the depth of citizen feeling about Watergate, and he and his party paid a heavy political price in the 1974 Congressional elections. Some believe that the pardon cost the President his own election in 1976.

Yet in his years in office, President Ford accomplished things such as the Helsinki Accords with the Soviet Union and thirty other nations, guaranteeing the integrity of national boundaries; a further easing of tensions with the People's Republic of China; and presiding over a recovery from economic recession. In sending American forces to rescue the Mayaguez, a ship seized by the Cambodians in 1975, President Ford demonstrated that our disappointment in Vietnam would not lead to our shrinking from the defense of ourselves and our principles.

To win the Republican nomination in 1976, President Ford beat back a strong challenge from Ronald Reagan, a very popular Republican politician in much of the country. His loss to Jimmy Carter in November was by the narrowest of margins; a swing of 29 electoral votes would have won Ford a full term.

In concluding his short speech on August 9, 1974, President Ford pledged "to do what is right as God gives me to see the right..." With these words from President Lincoln's second Inaugural Address, President Ford set out to "bind the nation's wounds," injuries different from those of civil war. Ford's successor, President Carter, began his speech by saying, "For myself and for our Nation, I want to thank my predecessor for all he has done to heal our land." Healing is often a gift from on high, for those who trust in the Lord.

Jimmy Carter

"He hath shewed thee, O man, what is good; and what doth the Lord require of thee, but to do justly, and to love mercy, and to walk humbly with thy God? (Micah 6:8) Fifty-six years before James Earl (Jimmy) Carter took the presidential oath with his hand on this chosen scripture, Warren Harding had used the same text to swear his oath. President Harding did not survive his term in office, and scandals litter the memory of his Presidency. Jimmy Carter fared better; he survived. But, Carter was only a one term President, an historical blip amidst 24 years of Republican domination of Presidential politics. Pundits slip easily into referring to the 39th President's administration as failed as well.

Pundits, of course, can be wrong. Consider the challenges; how does one do justly in the modern world without seeming judgmental or arrogant? Is loving mercy easily confused with weakness internationally and at home? How humbly can one walk as the leader of the most powerful nation on earth? Perhaps, in the second half of the 20th century, "failed" presidencies are more accurately described as unfulfilled great expectations.

The fact that Jimmy Carter took the oath on January 20, 1977 represents the convergence of remarkable political shrewdness and a unique moment in history. Carter brought many things to his Presidency, but experience on the national, let alone the international, scene was not one of them. How ironic, then, that the greatest success and biggest failure remembered by most Americans who knew his Presidency were both drawn from international affairs: the Camp David Accords and the Iranian hostage crisis. He got to Washington, though, by virtue of a campaign well-conceived to take advantage of the political realities.

Jimmy Carter began his adult life in the nuclear submarine program as an officer-graduate of the Naval Academy. When his father died, Carter returned to his home state of Georgia to run the family farm. He emerged naturally as a leader in local affairs and in 1962 decided to challenge the militantly-segregationist machine of the sitting state senator, using a court decision to engineer an upset. In 1970, he won the Georgia Governor's chair. His rapid move from leading citizen of Plains, Georgia to Governor in just eight years foretold his move to the national scene. Unable to succeed himself as Governor, Carter and his allies set out to capture the Democratic nomination in 1976, a goal first emerging in his mind in 1972.

How impossible a goal! No one from the deep South had been elected President since Zachary Taylor in 1848, and Taylor was a war hero. Small state governors carried no weight beyond their regions, if even there. A common campaign slight in 1976 (reminiscent of 1844 and Polk) was "Jimmy Who?" There were many more prominent Democrats nationally in 1975-76, and the Republicans had won a smashing electoral victory in 1972 with a tolerated-but-hardly-beloved Richard Nixon. They would offer either a very-popular Ronald Reagan or Gerald Ford, a safe choice, in 1976.

Watergate, however, had cost the Republicans the confidence of the electorate. President Ford's pardon of President Nixon, charitable and healing though it was, caused the wound of Watergate to fester a while longer.

Jimmy Carter presented a different look, a Southern politician without the political baggage of racism and segregation, a moderate Democrat in contrast to the overtly liberal Washington wing of the party. The early primary and caucus states were favorable venues for a populist from a small Southern state. In words which were prophetic, one aide described the campaign strategy as "we'll win in Iowa, New Hampshire and Florida and let *Time*, *Newsweek* and *U.S. News* do the rest." The early wins produced the bandwagon effect, amply aided by the media attention directed at the political story of the year. Following a time when criticism of an "imperial Presidency" was fresh in the minds of voters, the image of a man of the people, a peanut farmer, played well, especially because it seemed genuine.

President Carter also brought to office a history of participation in his church. When he returned to Plains after his naval service, Carter became a deacon at the Plains Baptist Church and began long service as a Bible class instructor. In his church life came an early indication that he might be a different kind of Southern Democrat. In 1964, he voted to invite black people to worship with whites at the church. In the context of that place and time, Carter's vote was noteworthy.

Throughout his campaign, media made much of his conservative Christian beliefs. His most devastating political gaffe in the campaign of 1976 resulted from his unguarded reference in religious terms to having "lusted" in his heart in a magazine interview. The nation learned, though, from his Presidency and afterwards that Carter's religious faith translated into activity; the focus on human rights, peacemaking with the Israeli Prime Minister Begin and the Egyptian President Sadat; building houses with Habitat for Humanity.

President Carter took his oath on two Bibles, one used by President Washington, the other a gift from his mother, Lillian Carter. Both were opened to Micah and were held by his wife, Rosalyn. Following his address, one of the shorter ones in history, the President and Mrs. Carter surprised the crowd and worried the Secret Service by walking the route of the Inaugural Parade. Whether contrived or spontaneous, the gesture reinforced the idea that a different kind of political leader had emerged, the outsider, come to Washington, a man of the people.

Carter tackled tough issues as President: an oil embargo, the need for a national energy policy, the Soviet invasion of Afghanistan, the Panama Canal Treaty, peace in the Mideast. A characteristically humanitarian act, permitting the deposed Shah of Iran to come to the United States to obtain medical treatment needed for survival led to the crisis of the hostages held in the American Embassy in Teheran for 444 days. Persistent inflation plagued his term as well and in 1980, Ronald Reagan led a rejuvenated Republican Party to a decisive victory in the presidential election.

In his Inaugural Address, President Carter had quoted the passage from Micah in opening, calling the verse a timeless admonition. And so it has been in American history, given its use by Governor Winthrop in the 1630s as a vision for America. Near the close of the speech, President Carter acknowledged the difficulty of doing justly. He then expressed his hope that his time in office would be remembered for the nation's renewed "search for humility, mercy and justice." Given this application of Micah as a measure, history might well view the Presidency of Jimmy Carter not as a failure but different.

Ronald Reagan

" ...a settler pushes west and sings a song, and the song echoes out forever and fills the unknowing air...It is the American sound...That's our heritage; that is our song. We sing it still. For all our problems, our differences, we are together as of old, as we raise our voices to the God who is the author of this most tender music." These words from the concluding lines of President Ronald Reagan's second Inaugural Address capture major aspects in the speaker's life; theater, Americanism, the solitary hero in a movie western, and a frequently-expressed fundamental faith in God. Indeed, the whole of that address, delivered on January 21, 1985 to avoid conflict with the Dolphin-49er Super Bowl football game on the 20th, blends simple images from American history with calls to prayer and straightforward plans to reduce the size of federal government in an engaging and dramatic way. The actor-President played both roles with ease.

On both occasions, January 20, 1981 and again in 1985, President Reagan took the oath of office with his left hand resting on his mother's Bible, opened to 2 Chronicles 7:14. "If my people which are called by my name, shall humble themselves, and pray, and seek my face, and turn from their wicked ways; then I will hear from heaven, and will forgive their sin, and will heal the land." The same passage had been used, coincidentally, by the last President before Reagan to serve two full terms, Eisenhower. The healing theme played well in 1981. With the nation beset by persistent inflation and fractiousness over such foreign issues as the Iran hostage situation and the American boycott of the 1980 Olympics in Moscow as a protest over the Soviet invasion of Afghanistan, political discourse was confused and shrill. Reagan called for an "era of national renewal" with revitalized "faith and hope."

Such words are hardly uncommon in an Inaugural Address. But, from his early years, Reagan valued the example of his mother, a member of the Disciples of Christ brotherhood, who was beloved by all for her simple acts of doing good for others. Ronald Reagan made friends easily from the start and eagerly pursued the adulation of others. Being pleasant and kind to others honored his mother by emulating her.

Yet deep friendships were few. Reagan was more of a loner. His fondness for the use of radio, beginning with a career announcing baseball games in Illinois through his FDR-like presentations from the White House provide an apt image. Radio provides a very personal connection with others without intimacy. The western hero rode alone, too.

Reagan developed a love for reading newspapers as a child, a love transferred to the few books at home, Horatio Alger stories and the Bible. One of his biographers, Lou Cannon, noted the impact of his Bible-reading. "His speeches sparkle with Biblical quotations and he told David Frost in a 1968 interview that the historical character he admired most was Jesus Christ." [42] The Alger stories promoted the faith that every young boy could succeed in America, God's promised land, and especially out West. No wonder, then, that the adult Reagan could state with conviction that "the American sound" was authored by God. John Winthrop's "city on a hill" was still the chosen land and its people the chosen of the Lord.

President Reagan's acting career provided wonderful training for the leader who must embody the varying moods of the nation. His time in Hollywood also coincided with the tempest over alleged communist influence in the industry, and he developed into an effective anti-Communist crusader. For the future President, loyalty was a black and white issue, and the two superpowers were clear expressions of good and evil. Supporters called that clarity; detractors thought him simplistic. Analysts called it popular.

Reagan had been a Democrat for Nixon as late as 1960, but changed his party affiliation in 1962. By 1964, he was the most effective spokesman for conservative causes in the country, like reducing federal government and standing up to the communists abroad. A trio of wealthy California Republicans, A.C. Rubel of Union Oil, Henry Salvatori, of Western Geophysical, and Holmes Tuttle a businessman and car dealer, saw Reagan as a formidable opponent for the incumbent Governor, Edmund G. (Pat) Brown and helped to fund Reagan's victory over Brown in 1966. As Governor of California, Reagan had prominent standing in the national Republican Party, one which extended beyond the end of his second term in 1975. A strong but ultimately unsuccessful challenger for the Republican Presidential nomination in 1976, Reagan was the favorite in 1980 and won easily. Then he defeated Jimmy Carter in the November election. His re-election win in 1984, over Carter's Vice President Walter Mondale, was the greatest Republican landslide in U.S. history; forty-nine states chose him in the Electoral College.

As President, Reagan consistently repeated familiar themes. The Federal Government was intruding upon the freedom of the individual. A balanced budget works for families, so why not for a nation? The forces of evil reside in the Evil Empire, the Soviet Union. God blesses America, always has and always will as long as we "humble ourselves, pray and turn from our wicked ways."

That consistency of image did not always match actual policy. His budgets were always unbalanced and the growth of the national debt was unprecedented. Few Presidents have been as successful in negotiating with the forces of evil from Moscow. The U.S. under Reagan even opened doors of commerce with our supposed mortal enemy. Happily for Reagan, the accomplishments, however inconsistent with the message, worked to define the President in the eyes of the citizenry as a leader. Reagan left office with greater personal popularity than any President since Franklin Roosevelt. How important was that image of leadership?

More members of the Reagan Administration were forced from office by indictments and alleged improprieties than from any other administration. Presidents Grant and Harding are judged to have been failures because of scandals in their administrations, and President Nixon was forced to resign. Yet Reagan was untouched, earning the sobriquet, the *Teflon* President. Even the controversy over the Iran Contra affair, where Presidential aides defied the law to pursue their own diplomatic agenda, did not appreciably damage the President's standing with the people.

Perhaps the reason is as simple as Reagan's message. The President stood for something felt deeply over a long period of time, and he was skilled at communicating that in which he believed. Sure, accommodations to politics--the art of the possible--occurred, but the message remained constant and the messenger effective. The boy who made friends easily was hard to dislike. He became the settler, pushing west, singing the song he believed to be written by God. And the people believed, too

George Bush

George Bush became the first incumbent Vice President since Martin Van Buren in 1836 to be elected and inaugurated President. Like Van Buren, Bush followed a popular and heroic two-term President. And, like Van Buren, Bush served only one term, losing the election of 1992. All of the disappointment lay in the future, though, when on January 20, 1989, George Bush took the oath of office to become the 41st President of the United States.

A lifelong Episcopalian, President Bush swore the oath with his hand on two Bibles held by his wife, Barbara. One Bible was the Washington volume, used first in 1789 and frequently since, and the second was the Bush family Bible. Both were opened to Matthew 5, the Sermon on the Mount. Chief Justice William Rehnquist officiated on this unusually mild winter day (50 degrees) as the Republican Party extended its control over the Executive Branch of the government for four more years,

Like Eisenhower before him, President Bush opened his Inaugural Address with a prayer.

"Heavenly Father, we bow our heads and thank you for your love. Accept our thanks for the peace that yields this day and the shared faith that makes its continuance likely. Make us strong to do your work, willing to heed and hear Your will and write on our hearts these words: 'Use power to help people.' For we are given power, not to advance our own purposes, nor to make a great show in the world, nor a name.

There is but one just use of power, and it is to serve the people. Help us to remember it, Lord. Amen."

The prayer captured the tone of his address which the President used as a way to define himself apart from his predecessor. "America is never wholly herself unless she is engaged in high moral purpose. We as a people have such a purpose today. It is to make kinder the face of the nation and gentler the face of the world," said President Bush. Kinder and gentler became the code words picked up by the media to describe the aims of the new President; softer, less heroic words than those of President Reagan's yet seemingly fitting for the place and time. Indeed, the tone was very much in keeping with the message of the Beatitudes, the most well-known passages from the Sermon on the Mount.

President Bush came to office with a personal history matching the fondest dreams of a modern campaign manager. Born into the family of a U.S. Senator and self-made millionaire, Bush enjoyed the educational advantages of independent schooling and Yale University. Yet when World War Two came, he joined the Navy and became, at age 18, its youngest commissioned pilot. He flew 58 missions in the Pacific, was shot down, rescued, and decorated for heroism. Then he came back, married Barbara and moved to Texas to make his own fortune in oil.

Fourteen years after moving west, enjoying success in business, Bush took on his first political responsibility as Chairman of the Harris County Republican Party. In 1967, he began the first of two terms in the House of Representatives, service which helped him later in his relations with Congress. In 1971, President Nixon appointed Bush to be U.S. Ambassador to the United Nations, providing the future President with yet another network of experiences which would prove helpful later. Positions as Chairman of the Republican National Committee, first U.S. Ambassador to the People's Republic of China and Director of the Central Intelligence Agency rounded out a resume which blended economic success, personal heroism, political organizing and experience in both domestic and foreign politics.

In 1980, Bush ran for the Republican nomination for President, losing to Reagan but winning the nominee's offer to be the Vice Presidential candidate. As Vice President, he was actively engaged in the affairs of state, hardly the outsider many Vice Presidents in history have felt themselves to be.

The breadth of Bush's experience proved useful in his own Presidency. While Bush won a decisive victory over Governor Michael Dukakis of Massachusetts, the Democratic Party still maintained control of Congress. A crisis in the savings-and-loan industry, with many institutions failing, budget crises almost annually and a mounting trade deficit meant that President Bush needed to collaborate with Congress though it was Democratic.

The collapse of communism, symbolized by the destruction of the Berlin Wall, and the rising democratic movement in the Soviet Union dictated that President Bush would spend considerable time focused on foreign affairs. The Iraqi invasion of Kuwait, turned back by forces representing the United Nations but led by the United States presented the Commander-in-Chief with still another foreign crisis requiring the blending of diplomacy and force. By virtue of his background, President Bush knew many of the world leaders with whom he had dealt before coming to office. A particularly pleasing moment for the President came in 1990 when Bush enjoyed the honor of attending the summit meeting in Paris where the 45 year long Cold War was declared to be ended.

Friends and political allies consistently described Bush as knowing his own mind, guileless, calm and competent. Critics thought him too secretive, indecisive and out-of-touch with the common man. All agreed that the President was unashamedly patriotic, the kind of person to get goose bumps over the National Anthem sung especially well, in some respects a throwback to an earlier, less cynical time. The President fostered that connection with former times in his Address when he said, "The old ideas are new again because they are not old, they are timeless; duty, sacrifice, commitment and a patriotism that finds its expression in taking part and pitching in." To him, public duty was not a cheerless burden but an honor.

President Bush's inauguration featured the revival of a public reception at the White House, something not done since President Taft in 1909. Immediately following the ceremony at the Capitol, President Bush signed his first Executive Order declaring January 22, 1989 to be a National Day of Prayer and Thanksgiving. Then he and Mrs. Bush participated in the Inaugural Parade by walking a few blocks, like President and Mrs. Carter. The walk seemed spontaneous, a symbolic way to bridge the distance modern circumstances have placed between the President and the people.

But the distance remained. Though President Bush enjoyed dazzlingly high numbers in the political polls following the Iraqi war, he never developed the same personal connection with the electorate evident with President Reagan.

Taught at an early age by his mother not to brag, President Bush always seemed somewhat ill at ease promoting himself, and in the campaign of 1992, he stumbled badly. His younger opponent capitalized on his greater personal level of comfort with technology and with "pressing the flesh." Additionally, Bill Clinton's circumstances in early life weren't marked by privilege, so he seemed more like one of the people. Most importantly, the U.S. economy had not fully recovered from severe recession and, as always, the incumbent President was held responsible. Clinton defeated Bush in a race marked by the emergence of a third candidate, millionaire Ross Perot.

The kinder, gentler qualities called for by the President in 1989 often lost out to more clamorous and divisive political reality during the Bush years. But, the Beatitudes bless many virtues and comfort even those who are reviled. Perhaps President Bush out of office could once again find solace in the words upon which he swore his oath of office.

Bill Clinton

"Where there is no vision, the people perish." These words from Proverbs 29:18 were prominent in the inauguration day of William Jefferson (Bill) Clinton, 42nd President. Bill Clinton chose this passage to differentiate himself politically from his predecessor, who claimed to have "trouble with that vision thing." But he also meant to underscore a point understood by the former Presidents, and in fact, well-expressed by President Bush in 1989: "America is never wholly herself unless she is engaged in high moral principle." And on January 20, 1993, Bill Clinton laid out his vision for America as a nation renewing itself by acting on its idealism, acting on the strength of its ideas, and in the words of St. Paul, never "wearying in well-doing, for in due season we shall reap if we faint not." (Galatians 6:9)

President Clinton gained election in part because he understood what pundits call the "MTV generation." Clinton's style was engagingly personal, well-suited to small-group interactions which could be televised nationally, creating a feeling of intimacy not unlike that created by FDR in his Fireside Chats. Clinton spoke the language of the computer age and, as a man born a part of the Baby Boom generation of post-World War Two America, was persuasive in his call for a change of the guard, much like President Kennedy represented in succeeding President Eisenhower. He also understood the power of symbolism. Consequently, the inaugural festivities in 1993 included features which both validated tradition, for continuity's sake, and introduced newness to differentiate himself from the past.

Clinton arrived in Washington D.C. for the inauguration in a caravan of buses which started at Jefferson's home in Monticello, emphasizing the value Clinton placed in the democratic principles of the third President. Vividly, the President-elect had connected the 1990s with 1801. The journey to inauguration had not carried such symbolic importance in many years.

The third youngest President, Clinton asked the most widely known and venerated minister in the nation (and one often associated with Republican Presidents), Rev. Billy Graham, to deliver the invocation. Like Kennedy, Clinton invited a poet to read, but his choice, Maya Angelou, made clear his intention to be inclusive, in gender and race, in his administration. The *New York Times*, on January 21, 1993, described Inauguration Day as a "casual and intimate day" and the crowd succeeded in persuading the Clintons to walk in their parade, like Bush and Carter before.

Yet traditional forms remained. The President-elect took the oath of office with his hand on a Bible given him by his grandmother, following the lead of the Chief Justice, William Rehnquist, who once again wore the official skull cap seldom seen on justices except at inaugurations. The Bible was opened to Galatians 6; the press reported "that the verse Clinton chose was 8." "For he that soweth to his flesh shall of the flesh reap corruption; but he that soweth to the Spirit shall of the Spirit reap life everlasting." Of course, verse 9, cited by President Clinton in his address, was also on the page. For the President, spiritual things mattered, as well as good deeds. Then, like many before him, President Clinton thanked his predecessor for his service to the nation and proceeded to lay out how he hoped to lead the nation differently.

The road to the White House for Bill Clinton began in rural Arkansas where he was raised for some time by a single mother. An early hero was President Kennedy whom he met when he was a Boy's Nation delegate as a teenager. He proceeded through college and law school with ease, winning a Rhodes Scholarship for study at Oxford University along the way. Clinton taught law at the University of Arkansas before beginning his political career as the state's Attorney General. There followed five two-year terms as Governor of Arkansas and emergence as a figure of national political importance through a coalition of party men and women who called themselves New Democrats to set themselves apart from the more liberal wing of the party.

Raised a Baptist, Clinton seemed proud of his religious background and at ease among church people. His campaigns frequently featured Biblical references and allusions, and he developed a speaking style which some described as sermonizing. That ability to blend the religious and the political is well-illustrated by the opening line of his acceptance speech at the Democratic National Convention: "I come from a place called Hope." referring both to his political aim and his home town, Hope, Arkansas, with a word celebrated by St. Paul in his letters. And he closed his Inaugural Address with: "From this joyful mountaintop of celebration, we hear the call to service in the valley. We have heard the trumpets, we have changed the guard. And now each in our own way, and with God's help, we must answer the call."

President Clinton's Administration has included political battles over budgets, free trade, gays in the military and reform of the health care delivery system. Foreign affairs problems have challenged the nation as well; peacekeeping in Somalia, imposing our vision of democracy in Haiti, civil war in Bosnia. Allies of the President have applauded Clinton's willingness to tackle long-standing and controversial political issues such as health care. Critics have characterized him as indecisive and too willing to compromise his own political beliefs and the interests of America abroad. Sound historical judgment awaits. However, even if one does not believe that President Clinton has been engaged in "well-doing," all acknowledge that he has "not wearied."

In the Inauguration, there occurred once more a moment unique to this nation. Columnist R.W. Apple, in the *New York Times,* described it: "It was a day when the nation committed itself once more, with the recital of a simple 18th century oath, to what the new President termed 'the mystery of American renewal.' The solemn magic of the moment, in this most telling of national rituals, lies in what it symbolizes: the unquestioned acceptance by victor, vanquished and public alike of the continuity and legitimacy of governance." [43]

In the concept of our nation, in the manner of the transfer of political authority, there has, indeed, been vision, the vision of great minds long ago. And the people have not perished.

Conclusion

January 20, 1997 will bring the United States either a second term 42nd President or a 43rd to be inaugurated, barring intervening tragedy. Almost certainly, the individual will take the oath with a hand on the Bible, probably one opened to a favorite passage. Likely, the President will call upon Providence or God or the Divine Presence, whatever the term preferred, to guide the destiny of the nation as the nation has been guided in the past. Once more, the traditional connection between religious faith and political works will be made without much concern that the Bill of Rights separation of church and state might be compromised.

Indeed, the connection the President makes is consistent with the history and character of our country. Understanding the United States also requires a comprehension of its religious history. Americans of the 1990s who see in the prominence of the so-called "religious right" an unprecedented intrusion into political life by religious forces only show their limited knowledge of the past three centuries. If, as President Bush contended, America is never so fully herself as when engaged in high moral purpose, so those purposes have never been much separated from the dominant religious principles of the nation. And, these principles have been regularly and consistently expressed. Nineteenth century social reform movements and twentieth century Progressivism are but two examples of political movements owing life to religious roots.

As a nation, we have taken Governor Winthrop's dream of a city on a hill seriously. We believe our political system to be preferable to all others and have actively worked to export democracy. Likewise, our faith in a capitalist, free enterprise economic system has been a part of U.S. exports during the course of our history. We have conducted ourselves as a chosen people, and we have enjoyed unparalleled prosperity in both economic and political terms, reinforcing our belief in our chosen-ness. To be mindful of the possibility that prosperity, whether individual or national, might be in part the result of the blessings of God has become as important to the rituals of the transfer of political power as the orderliness of the process itself.

Some of our Presidents have been more openly religious than others. Some have possessed greater knowledge of the Bible; others have searched for religious truth outside traditional denominations. All have worked to "do justly and love mercy" insofar as they have understood what these "requirements" of God mean.

In nearly every instance, the unity noted clearly by R.W. Apple and William Safire as the defining quality in the inaugural act has quickly fractured under the stress of practical politics. History books tell of good deeds and bad, noble actions and mean-spirited ones, high moral purposes and coarsely political ones. Inaugurations are a moment of cleansing when we all say we hope to be better, individually and as a nation, in our interactions with others. Often we fail yet sometimes we don't. Through our Presidents in their proud and humbling moment of inauguration, we pledge to keep on trying to be worthy of being the city on the hill, to do justly and to love mercy. So help us God!

Endnotes

1. William Safire and Leonard Safir, *Words of Wisdom*, Fireside, New York, 1989, p. 252.
2. William Safire, *The New York Times*, January 21, 1985.
3. James Thomas Flexner, *Washington: The Indispensible Man*, New American Library, New York, 1974, p. 216.
4. Page Smith, *John Adams*, Doubleday, Garden City, NY, 1962, p. 1078.
5. Smith, p. 917.
6. Thomas Jefferson to Rev. Jeremy Belknap, in *The Jefferson Bible*, Beacon Hill, Boston, 1989, p. 8.
7. Garry Wills, *Under God*, Simon and Schuster, New York, 1990, p. 376.
8. Daniel. C. Gilman, *James Monroe*, Houghton Mifflin, New York, 1899, p. 249.
9. Gilman, p. 245.
10. Gilman, p. 245.
11. Glenn D. Kittler, *Hail to the Chief*, Chilton Books, Philadelphia, 1968, p. 35.
12. Kittler, pp. 33-35.
13. Paul F. Boller, Jr., *Presidential Anecdotes*, Penguin, New York, 1981, p. 57
14. *Family Encyclopedia of American History*, Reader's Digest Books, Pleasantville, NY, 1975. p. 9.
15. Boller, p. 57.

16. John William Ward, *Andrew Jackson: Symbol for an Age*, Oxford U. Press, New York, 1962, p. 195, quoting Samuel A. Cartwright eulogy for Jackon, July 12, 1845, Natchez, Mississippi.
17. Kittler, p. 44.
18. Kittler, p. 51.
19. Robert Seager II, *and Tyler Too*, McGraw Hill, New York, 1963, p. 310.
20. John M. Blum, et. al., *The National Experience*, 6th Edition, Harcourt Brace Jovanovich, San Diego, 1985, p. 276.
21. Robert J. Rayback. *Millard Fillmore*, Henry Stewart Publishers, Buffalo, New York, 1959, p. 271.
22. Rayback, p. 407.
23. Family Encyclopedia, p. 869.
24. Garry Wills, *Lincoln at Gettysburg*, Simon and Schuster, New York, 1992, p. 185.
25. Boller, p. 147, quoting James S. Jones, in *The Life of Andrew Johnson*, Greenville, Tennessee, 1911, pp. 27-28.
26. Lately Thomas, *The First President Johnson*, William Morrow, New York, 1968. p. 49.
27. Thomas, p. 60.
28. Kittler, p. 116.
29. Boller, p. 175.
30. *New York Times*, March 5, 1885.
31. ibid.
32. *New York Times*, March 5, 1889
33. Kittler, p. 149.
34. *New York Times*, March 5, 1913.
35. The details of the room and ceremony are taken from the *New York Times*, August 4, 1923.
36. *New York Times*, January 21, 1937.
37. David McCullough, *Truman*, Simon and Schuster, New York, 1992, p.347.
38. ibid.
39. Dwight Eisenhower, *Mandate for Change*, Signet Books, New York, 1963, p. 139.
40. Kittler, p. 217.
41. TerHorst, *Gerald Ford*, The Third Pres, New York, 1974, p. 139.

42. Lou Cannon, *Ronnie and Jesse*, Doubleday and Company,
    Garden City, New York, 1969, p. 5.
43. *New York Times*, January 21, 1993.

About the author

Daniel E. White earned his Ph.D. at the University of California, Riverside in 1973. His dissertation focused on the Eisenhower Administration. Following administrative and teaching positions at UCR and the University of Southern Colorado, he was Headmaster of the Webb School of California. He currently serves as the Head of Sacramento Country Day School and is an Adjunct Professor for the University of Southern California, School of Public Policy, Sacramento Center. He and his wife, Judy, live in Fair Oaks, California.